POUND *for* POUND

POUND

for

POUND

A Story of One Woman's Recovery
and the Shelter Dogs Who Loved Her
Back to Life

SHANNON KOPP

WILLIAM MORROW
An Imprint of HarperCollins*Publishers*

POUND FOR POUND. Copyright © 2015 by Shannon Kopp. All rights reserved. Printed in the United States of America. No part of this book may be used or reproduced in any manner whatsoever without written permission except in the case of brief quotations embodied in critical articles and reviews. For information address HarperCollins Publishers, 195 Broadway, New York, NY 10007.

HarperCollins books may be purchased for educational, business, or sales promotional use. For information please e-mail the Special Markets Department at SPsales@harpercollins.com.

FIRST EDITION

Designed by Fritz Metsch

Library of Congress Cataloging-in-Publication Data has been applied for.

ISBN 978-0-06-237022-8

15 16 17 18 19   OV/RRD   10 9 8 7 6 5 4 3 2 1

Dedicated to Julie—
my sister, my joy, my inspiration,
my heart.

AUTHOR'S NOTE

THIS IS A true story constructed from my memory and personal journals. I've changed the names and identifying characteristics of some people who appear in my book. I have also withheld the name of an animal shelter and changed some orienting details associated with it, so as not to create controversy that might impact their vital fund-raising efforts.

In 1984, an estimated 17 million animals were killed every year in America's shelter system. Today, thanks to the hard work of many animal lovers, and organizations like Best Friends Animal Society, that number has decreased to 4 million. Still, the tragic reality remains that 9,000 dogs and cats are euthanized daily in U.S. shelters.

I'd like to thank the many shelter staff and volunteers I've met over the years, from veterinarians to humane investigations officers to animal caregivers to humane educators, who are working tirelessly to end the suffering and euthanasia of adoptable animals in America. You are true heroes, warriors of the heart. May your passion, courage, and dedication live on every day.

PART ONE

Once a young woman said to me, "Hafiz, what is the sign of someone who knows God?"

I became very quiet, and looked deep into her eyes, then replied,

"My dear, they have dropped the knife. Someone who knows God has dropped the cruel knife

that most so often use upon their tender self and others."

—HAFIZ, *"Once a Young Woman Said to Me,"*
translated by Daniel Ladinsky

I

YEARS BEFORE ALCOHOLISM destroyed my father, when I was still a small child, I would roar and meow and quack and moo. He would film me while I got on my hands and knees and pretended to be a dog or beat my chest like a monkey or puckered my lips like a fish. I wanted to be Jane Goodall when I grew up. Near my bed, I kept a picture of her touching the fingertips of a chimp. On my shelves, I kept all her books. No one called me crazy.

I knew, with that childlike clarity that doesn't consider what makes sense, that I was destined to spend a lot of time with animals and that this would make me live happily well past the ever after. I never dreamed of growing up to become a rock-bottom bulimic, a person swallowed by a ceaseless desire to fill up and get empty.

But I suppose the only future in a child's dream is a good one.

When I first stuck my hands down my throat at seventeen, I wanted to lose some weight. Animals couldn't make the guys I liked like me back. Animals couldn't make me fit in with the popular girls. Animals couldn't keep my father sober. Animals couldn't give me the things I needed to be okay.

I believed power and love accompanied a thinner body.

But the things you believe can be a choke chain. They can steal from your dreams, your dignity, your ability to care for yourself and others.

What you believe can steal your life.

WHEN I WAS eighteen, I participated in a homemade bikini contest in Springfield, Massachusetts, dead sober, at a club called, ironically, the Hippodrome. My best friend, Chloe, was doing this contest and in my eyes, she had the perfect body, the perfect face, the perfect style. I wanted to be just like her. So I didn't flinch when a middle-aged woman with huge breasts in a tube top asked me to sign up, too.

The emcee introduced Chloe as "One Yummy Treat" and she strutted onstage in front of a crowd of a hundred clubgoers, with just a few Reese's Peanut Butter Cup wrappers taped to her naked body. She slathered herself in whipped cream, squatted, and smacked the floor with her hands. When the audience went wild, a panic came over me. I was wearing two cupcake wrappers taped over my nipples and one over my crotch, nothing covering my ass. My legs, freshly shaven and doused in oil to make them glisten under the spotlight, wouldn't move.

"Birthday Surprise," the emcee called, and a black girl dressed in every color of the rainbow tapped me on the shoulder and said, "You're up."

The stage vibrated beneath my feet while speakers boomed Juvenile's "Back That Azz Up." Pink and blue lights beamed like lasers around the room, and the crowd whistled and hooted. The louder the crowd became, the more the rush of feeling desired exhilarated me, the more I grinded and shook my ass.

I came in second. I beat the girl who wore just a garden hose over her body and a sunflower in her hair. I beat the one covered in liquefied chocolate. I beat the rainbow girl, too, and I was thrilled. I went back to the prop room beaming with pride. Looking good, without a doubt, was worth it.

The prop room was small and dimly lit, filled with piles of fake flowers, glitter, whipped cream cans, and pinwheels. While I unpeeled the cupcake wrappers from my body to get dressed, a colony of black ants swarmed around some cake crumbs in the corner of the room. Other girls took shots, put their six-inch heels back on. I watched a dozen inky black specks trek in single file with cake crumbs on their backs. They disappeared and reemerged from a small hole in the wall, focused only on their mission, clueless about their fragility, how they could drown in a wad of spit or be smashed by a finger in two seconds.

Where were the ants putting these crumbs? Why were they always in search of more?

WHEN I THINK back to the girl in that prop room, I wish I could tell her to find stable ground, to stay away from anything that told her the size of her body mattered, whether in a magazine or in a crowd of throbbing dicks and clapping hands at the Hippodrome or anywhere in the known world. I wish I could tell her to stay close to the things she loved. *Find joy*, I would say. *Feel alive!*

But I didn't know how. My father drowned in seas of vodka and denial. I stuck my fingers down my throat and reached all the way to my heart, trying to yank it out. I didn't know that the dark hole in my life wasn't in some wall but was instead deep inside me, an endless urge for more. I didn't know that in five years I would be hospitalized and living in a rehab center with women who were too thin to walk, only allowing themselves to eat things like computer paper and miniature carrots. I didn't know that I would wake up with raw knuckles, bloodshot eyes, and the feeling that my throat was on fire, and that would be normal. For eight years, I grew sicker and sicker until I was vomiting up to twenty times a night.

Every morning, I believed I could make a choice to be sane around food and eat like a normal person. I believed I could make a choice not to lie or hurt the people I loved. I vowed to do better, for my mother, for my sister, for myself, but by noon, those promises were in the toilet. My whole life was.

NOT LONG AGO, on a Saturday morning, I volunteered at a local animal shelter. I brought a black pit bull to the play yard behind the shelter, which wasn't really a play yard but a slab of urine-stained concrete surrounded by pebbles and bushes. The dog didn't have a name since she came in as a stray, but I named her Midnight.

Her rear wagged so forcefully that it moved her lower half from side to side. I opened the back door and unleashed her into the yard, and she took off in a full sprint. She rocketed from one end of the small space to the other, galloping back and forth and sometimes leaping into the air. Joy radiated from every ounce of her muscular body. She was a force of wild energy, an intensity of aliveness.

"Midnight, slow down, girl," I said while she charged past.

"Hey, don't go too crazy!" I yelled, and she stopped in her tracks. She turned her head back to look at me as if to say, *Don't you understand? This is all there is!*

She began to run in wide circles around me with her tongue

out, lips pushed back, ears flapping in the wind, without an ounce of complaint or fear in her eyes.

The temperature was in the eighties, and her chest was heaving, so I unraveled the hose. I turned the water on and Midnight trotted over to slurp up the stream. When she was finished, I put my thumb over the spigot and the water sprayed like a fountain, the mist glistening in the sunlight and landing on her black coat.

Midnight stood there so still, so utterly delighted, her neck tilted up, eyes closed, mouth open. She let each drop of water fall onto her tongue as if it were a snowflake falling from the sky.

THAT NIGHT I dreamt of Midnight and that I was a child again. My hair was long and blond, my face was pink with excitement, my body was beautifully unimportant.

Midnight was the size of a horse, and I lay on her back with my arms wrapped around her neck, my head pressed against the top of hers. She ran across a sunflower field and I slept on top of her. In my dream, she ran and ran and ran until her coat turned yellow. I didn't wake up until she stopped running and tilted her nose to the sun, chest heaving like it had in the play yard, her nostrils working overtime, her tongue out and mouth wide like a smile.

The next time I went to the shelter, I found out that Midnight was gone. She had been euthanized.

THIS BOOK IS my love letter to her, and to every shelter dog who, by their own nature, communicates in the most honest language I've ever known. If a dog wants to be left alone, she keeps her distance. If she is afraid, she trembles. If she wants love, she pushes her nose through the bars and reaches for it. She leaps into your arms. She greets you with an enthusiasm that seems like it doesn't belong in such a dark, barren place.

Midnight knew that she didn't belong in a cage, separated from the sights, sounds, and smells of the world that made her feel alive. You wouldn't find her owning her captivity or making herself comfortable. You wouldn't find her pretending that things weren't so bad or accepting how small her life had become. You'd find Midnight at the front of her pen, pushing her nose through the bars, saying, *I was meant for more.*

I never thought I was meant for more. Sometimes I still don't. My hands are out of my throat, but I can still look at my body and call it fat. I can still get swallowed up in depression. I can still look at what happened to Midnight and somehow blame myself. I can still think, *You're thirty and don't know what you're doing with your life. You are too old to miss your dad as much as you do.* I can think, *You need to be stronger. Braver. You need to change your life.*

But then I put on a pair of ripped jeans and a T-shirt and wash the makeup off my face and pull my hair back. I go to the shelter, which sometimes feels like the only part of the earth that sustains me, the only place I can lie down in the dirt and say, "I'm not ready to change. I'm not ready to change."

The dogs don't judge me or give me a motivational speech. They don't rush me to heal or grow. They don't talk me up or put me down. They sit in my lap and lick my face and make me feel chosen.

And sometimes, it hits me hard that I'm doing the exact thing I say I cannot do.

Changing.

2

SCIENTISTS SAY THAT when earth was formed 4.5 billion years ago, the lighter materials like water and air rose to the surface, while the heaviest elements sank to the middle of the planet, where they formed the center of earth, the inner core, a blazing metallic ball so powerful it can change the location of the magnetic north and south poles and can support weights beyond the human imagination. Without the inner core, Mount Everest, let alone the rest of the world, would collapse.

In the geology of our hearts, it is often one person who holds the most emotional energy. This person makes our world spin and supports our great weight, and without this person's love, we'd crumble.

We all have an inner core.

For many years, my father was mine.

I LOVED HIM in all the ways little girls love their fathers, but I was convinced that, out of all the amazing, lovable fathers in the world, my dad was the best. He wasn't just the life of the party; he was the life of the neighborhood, the playground, the basketball court, the black Nissan Maxima. He could make a quick trip to the grocery store a rocking concert. When he was driving, I never sat in boredom, playing with my hair and looking out the window. With the windows rolled down, I'd pretend I had an air guitar or that my knees were drums and belt out the Counting Crows or the Beatles along with him, singing so loud my throat got hoarse.

And then at night, he often threw a party just for the two of us, blaring "Walk the Dinosaur" or "Love Shack" on the stereo, carrying me on his shoulders so that we were like one body. One big dancing machine. Up and down the stairs. Around the dining room table. Down the deck stairs and into the backyard. I'd wave my hands wildly while he broke it down below, Mom following us around, laughing her head off.

We lived in a brand-new two-story home in the suburban town of South Windsor, Connecticut. My parents moved in before I was born, when Dad was at the start of a successful twenty-year sales career at a tax software company. He had met my mother eight years earlier, when he was studying business at the University of Connecticut and she was an insurance agent in Hartford. Mom was a bold and gorgeous woman, and she did what made her happy without caring what other people thought about it. On her wedding day, she chopped off her long, silky brown hair to "surprise" my father. She could do things like that, rock a supershort haircut or wear orange stripes and red polka dots, and still look stunning.

When Mom wasn't taking care of my sister and me, she did volunteer work or made dinners for friends or neighbors or family who were going through difficult times. Mom didn't worship the Catholic God my father did, but she believed in Kindness. She believed in Love over hate, no matter what. She believed that everyone, regardless of how far they'd fallen, deserved a second chance. And sometimes a third and a fourth and a fifth.

She also believed in Vacations.

Once every summer, until I was sixteen, we stayed at a lake cabin for a week, boating and barbecuing with Dad's college friends and their kids, with whom I was raised like family. During the winter, Dad's company paid for our family to go to Hawaii or Florida or California—warm, bright, glistening places where we could hike mountains and kiss dolphins on the lips and go boogie boarding and eat at fancy restaurants and dance to live music all we wanted.

Wherever we were, I paired off with Dad every chance I got. We skied steeper slopes than my mother and sister. We rode roller coasters while Mom and Julie stuck to Ferris wheels and water rides. We celebrated our birthdays together since they were just a few weeks apart. We storm watched. We saw Broadway plays together in New York, and went to the Hard Rock Café afterward to eat chocolate cake. We watched UConn men's and women's basketball games with husky dogs painted on our faces.

No matter what we were doing, I always wanted to make him proud. I skied slopes I wasn't ready for and rode rides that terrified me because I wanted him to think I was brave. At my soccer games, I ran much harder if Dad was in the stands. In school, I worked tirelessly to get A's so that he would think I was smart. And eventually, I began to work very hard on my appearance, so that Dad would call me pretty.

When I succeeded, he was so loud with his pride, so beaming and boastful and ridiculously happy. My sister and I were his beautiful girls. The lights of his life. He looked for every reason to brag about us. He still does today. I could write three words—"I miss you"—and he'd declare them worthy of a Pulitzer.

"How much do I love you?" he would ask when I was a child.

"You love me two billion and two," I would say.

For years, I thought this was the biggest number in the world. And just like it never even occurred to me that there could be a two billion and three, it never occurred to me that my inner core, my Daddy, would implode.

MY FIRST CHILDHOOD memory is when I was four and playing "The Babies Are Crying!" with Dad, a game he invented. It was sometime after Dad got home from work, but still light out. The sun radiated in through the skylights and into the family room, casting a warm beam of light across the coffee table. Dad and I laid my Cabbage Patch dolls, Samantha and Kassie, on the couch as gently as possible so as not to wake them.

He kissed the dolls on the forehead. Then he kissed me on the cheek.

"Oh, thank God, Samantha and Kassie are finally asleep!" he said, and that was my cue to follow him, tiptoeing into the kitchen. I wasn't as tall as his waist yet, and I wore my favorite Little Mermaid pajamas. My hair was blond, almost white. His was brown, nearly black. He wore Adidas workout pants and a white T-shirt, which made his tan from his last business trip to Bermuda seem even darker.

We both sat down at the kitchen table and waited. My feet didn't touch the floor. I kicked them back and forth in the air. My body tingled in anticipation. Sometimes I thought I couldn't do it. But I waited. Because I knew he'd do it. He always did. And after a few painfully long seconds, I heard him begin to inhale a deep breath that could only mean one thing. He placed both hands on the sides of his face. He gasped and we both jumped out of our chairs.

"The babies are crying!" he shouted as we ran into the family room. I picked up Samantha and he got Kassie. We put their heads over our shoulders and said, "There, there," patting their backs.

"Do you think they need more milk?" I asked Dad.

"No, I think they are sick," he said.

I felt Samantha's hard head with the back of my palm. "Oh no, it's a fever!"

"Yes, a fever," Dad confirmed. "And the measles. I'll call the doctor right now."

His left hand became an imaginary phone that he put to his ear. "Hello? Yes, Kassie and Samantha. Yep. Okay? Twice a day? You got it."

I sat on the edge of the couch with the amount of concern one might have about potentially losing a leg. My lips pinched together and eyes widened.

"What did the doctor say?" I asked.

Dad took a painfully slow and serious breath. Then he picked up the remote control and held it like a precious gem.

"You see this?" he said. "It's special milk. Put it to her mouth like this and make sure she drinks all of it. Then she will feel better."

He put the remote to Kassie's ever-parted lips and said a few seconds later, "Look, sweetie, it's working!"

"Thank God!" I said, a phrase I sometimes heard Dad say when the UConn Huskies took the lead in a basketball game.

I gave my doll the special milk, too.

"Phew," I said. "That was a close one."

It was always a close one.

Then Dad and I put the dolls back to sleep and tiptoed back to the kitchen, where I took a seat across the table from him, waiting, sensitive to his every move, until finally, he gasped and yelled, "The babies are crying!"

And we did it all over again.

TODAY AS I write this, my father still walks around the world breathing and answering to the same name, but the light in his eyes is gone, and the voice that was once so loud and confident is now filled with anxious doubt, and every other time I see him, which is not often, I find myself bawling in a corner five minutes later. Alcoholism has killed him in every way but physically.

Dad began binge drinking in secret when I was in middle school, and crossed the line into full-blown alcoholism sometime when I was in high school. To this day, I can't pinpoint exactly why. He had been a social drinker, just like everyone our family knew, but something inside him flipped the alcohol switch, and he was never the same again.

The day I finally understood the reason my parents were fighting so much and Dad was locking the door to his office and coming home less and less, I was sixteen. Dad put as much energy into hiding his drinking as he did scoring big promotions at work, but still, part of me wonders why it took me so long to see the obvious signs of alcohol abuse: slurred speech; falling asleep on the floor; frequent, unexpected absences; screaming matches between my parents. Another part of me knows just how appealing the game of pretend has always been to me. I was never looking to find anything wrong with the father I so adored, and ultimately, I wouldn't until I was forced to.

· ·   ·

IT HAPPENED ON a Tuesday. I woke up and flossed gunk out of my braces and tried to flatten my unruly hair and went to school and sucked at math and fell in love with another book and kissed my sweet boyfriend and rode the school bus home and walked through the front door of my big beautiful house. I dropped my backpack in the corner of our spacious foyer and Sugar, our seven-year-old bichon frise, danced in circles around my feet. She jumped up on her hind legs, waving her front paws and wagging her tail like I'd been gone for ten years. Then she threw her head back and barked, the signature "Sugar howl," a throaty, grumbly sound that went up octaves the longer she did it. She was fifteen pounds with white, curly hair, and so much joy in her black button eyes that nobody, not even Oscar the Grouch, could look at her and keep a frown on.

I took dance classes four days a week in high school and taught tap to kids, so I ran upstairs to change. Sugar followed me, her pink dog tags jingling with every step, her toenails sliding on the wood stairs.

But on the way to my bedroom, I heard a strange sound down the hall, a sound like an animal groaning. I went to my parents' room and found Dad sprawled out on his back on the bed. He wore only a pair of white underwear and black socks. His eyes were closed. His cheeks and forehead and neck looked a sickly salmon pink. Drool dripped down his chin.

I ran to him and jumped onto the bed and knelt down by his head. Sugar jumped up, too, climbing onto his stomach, which made him groan again. Sugar's ears pricked and then they flattened to the top of her head. Her tail stopped wagging.

I shoved Sugar off Dad and wrapped my arms around him.

I begged him to open his eyes. I tried to lift the dead weight of his upper body. I dug my fingers into the skin of his shoulders and shook him. "Wake up!" I screamed.

He opened his bloodshot eyes for just a moment, then closed them. Red veins filled the whites of his eyes, crowding in on black pupils that were cloudy and looking off into nowhere.

Dad grabbed my hand so tightly it hurt. I gulped down a cry. He pulled me close to his face and a gust of thick, alcohol-soaked air hit my nose.

"I'm fine," he slurred.

I was stunned by the words and the smell and the slur and the fact that Dad was drunk, not dying.

The front door to the house opened. Sugar leapt off the bed and ran to greet my mother. My heart pounded in my chest while I yelled for Mom and stared out the window overlooking our backyard, the woods fading from lime-green colors to earth tones, limp and shimmering after a spring shower.

Mom burst through the door wearing a black business suit with her heels still on. She had just finished a long day working at an insurance agency ten minutes down the road.

"Oh Jeffrey," she said while she sat down on the bed, still catching her breath.

Mom seemed mad but not too freaked-out, as though it wasn't time to call 911 and she'd seen this before. My knees were against the side of Dad's body, my hand still in his warm hand. I looked at her. "What is going on?" I said.

She tucked a strand of my hair behind my ear and sighed. I couldn't tell if she was about to yell or cry.

She turned to my father and snapped. "Are you happy now? Now that your daughter has seen you like this?"

"No," he cried softly. Then he turned to look at me. "No, I'm not," he whispered under his vodka breath.

I felt his shame, like it was a living, breathing beast, but he was a fog of a man. There was no light in his eyes. In him.

He looked up at me and said, "Baby, I'm fine." He began sobbing then, almost as if he were chanting his misery.

"No, you're not fine," I said. "But you will be."

I said this with the confidence of a person who knew nothing about the allure of fading out of this world and into another, a world that numbs and blurs. You exit your life and the things you promised yourself you'd do today and the people counting on you. You free-fall into the dark, declaring with dangling legs and flailing arms: *tomorrow, tomorrow is the day I land.*

FROM THAT DAY on, my father became one of two things: a man desperate to get sober, or a man desperate to get drunk, with much more desperation expended on the latter.

Over the next decade, Dad became a ghostlike presence, disappearing for weeks, bouncing in and out of rehabs and hospitals, and eventually, landing himself in an orange jumpsuit behind bars after a drunk driving accident, writing me long letters of love. Letters of apology. Letters of regret. Letters of him still calling me his beautiful girl.

I'd stare down at his clean handwriting, the words I knew came from some sincere place deep inside him beneath all the lies and the booze, and sometimes, it felt like Rome's Colosseum fell down on my own heart, something ancient and enormous and broken crushing my insides, and the only way I could stop feeling the pain would be to pretend it wasn't happening. And so I became very good at that.

There were girls who lost their dads for real. Heart attacks. Cancer. Strokes. Car accidents. I'd think about these girls haunted by funerals and ashes and all the people who didn't know what to say or said the wrong things, and I'd think, *Now, that is awful. Mind-blowingly, gut-wrenchingly awful.* I told myself what I was dealing with was nothing. My life was cake compared to theirs. At least my dad was still alive. Even if he was a drunk, I could at least have some hope.

But hope isn't always a flame one should keep burning, an inspiration, a beautiful thing never to give up on. Sometimes hope is denial's sidekick. Sometimes it's the very thing that keeps you trapped in your misery, living for tomorrow, refusing to accept the suckiness of right now.

In my world, hope didn't float. Hope didn't inspire. Hope was the reason I never allowed myself to grieve. To feel. To acknowledge just how sick and far gone my father was, and later, how sick and far gone I was.

Emily Dickinson wrote, "'Hope' is the thing with feathers."

I thought she was full of shit—hope is the thing that lies.

But someday, I'd realize my truth.

Hope is a wet, black nose.

3

DURING MY FINAL years of high school, Dad began drinking at home more. I got used to finding bottles hidden around the house and Dad passed out. Often when I woke him up, he shook with sobs, snot dripping down his chin and lips, apologies slurring out of his mouth. Sometimes he needed to go to the hospital. Sometimes he just slept it off.

Dad wasn't angry or unpredictable when he drank. He was angry and unpredictable when sober. I don't have a single memory of my father screaming at me as a child, but throughout high school, the more he battled alcoholism's endless demons, the more I began to dread his chilling almond eyes. One night, he yelled at my sister and me for using too much floss with so much seriousness you would have thought we'd used the last remains of water during a drought. Whenever I asked to have my friends over, he roared about how selfish I was, that I didn't appreciate anything he did. Sometimes when he caught sight of me in my dance clothes, he reminded me how much money he'd shelled out for dance all my life, and what an expensive and unappreciative kid I was.

Had this rage always lived inside him? Had he always been a volcano waiting to erupt? Was everything I'd ever believed about him a lie?

I didn't know. What I knew was that I hated him for mor-phing from the love that raised me into a monster I could never please. But, more than that, I hated the fact that I couldn't please him.

There were many loud and tearful fights between my parents. Mom came close to kicking Dad out several times, but he reminded her of her sister Diane, who struggled with bipolar disorder. Mom often told me how much she loved Diane, how she was one of the most beautiful people she ever knew, but something happened when Diane turned seven-teen, something no one could fully understand. She began to fluctuate between manic and depressive states, and quickly became unrecognizable from the big sister she'd been to my mother growing up. The disease lived in her mind, my mother said. Diane could not control it. Medicine could not control it. No one could. It was a disease as fatal as cancer. Diane fought hard for almost two decades. But in the end, it drove her to suicide.

Mom knew that Dad didn't suffer from bipolar disorder, but as all rational and medical approaches continued to fail, she came to see addiction as a kind of mental illness. Eventually, she would realize her powerlessness over his alcoholism and divorce him after I finished college, but in the beginning, she refused to give up on him, bringing him to doctor after doctor, rehab after rehab. She had married him to have and to hold in sickness and in health, and he was very, very sick.

WHILE MOM EXERTED most all her energy in trying to rescue Dad, I focused on the superficial. Making things beautiful. Making me beautiful.

I had gotten my period late in life (age sixteen) and all at once, my dance leotards seemed to grow tighter in my chest and hips. My reflection had never bothered me before, but now, for two or three hours at a time in dance class, I saw a pimply horse doing pirouettes in the mirror.

Perhaps every teenage girl feels like she is one big problem in need of fixing, but I began to feel that way more than ever as my family fell apart. And it was easier to blame my unhappiness on my appearance rather than something I couldn't understand or explain.

So I began trying to "fix" my frumpy clothes with designer jeans, to clear my zitty chin with Oxy pads, and to tame my hair with products that made frizz seem like a serious emergency: "Real Control Intense Renewal Super Moisturizing Masks," and "Nexxus Emergencee Strengthening Polymeric Reconstructor," and on and on.

Bottles and creams and masks piled up in the bathroom like some mad scientist's laboratory. Then came the concealers and bronzers and primers and lipstick and eyeliners and mascara. Then came the "Very Sexy Push-Up Bra" from Victoria's Secret, clothes from Abercrombie & Fitch, and monthly passes to Sun City Tanning and Cardio World, a twenty-four-hour gym. There was an addictive quality to my ongoing makeover . . . always more to buy, more to do, and all that shallow "doing" quickly began to gnaw at my soul.

Some part of me craved that gnawing, that suffering. It felt oddly productive. Like I was erasing not only this uncool idea of myself on the outside, but all the ugliness within—the hatred I felt for my father and myself and whatever cruel kind of God would sit back and watch my family crumble.

The big lie I bet my life on was that I could somehow tone or wear or moisturize or buy my way to a happier, more comfortable existence, a place where everything was finally, permanently okay. Maybe even a little more than okay. Maybe even perfect, like the glossy ads said it could be.

MOM WAS LESS than pleased about my new grooming tools ("Why on earth do you need an eyelash curler?!"), but Sugar was thrilled about them. She discovered right away just how much she enjoyed watermelon-flavored lip gloss, and on more than one occasion, when I left my makeup bag unzipped on the floor near a full-length mirror in my bedroom, she squeezed almost all of the shimmery goo out of its tube. Gloss covered Sugar's white muzzle, and even clumped on the top of her head like hair gel, and when she pooped, it glittered a little.

One winter night, when I caught her pulling out an expensive bronzer blush from my makeup bag, I yelled at her and called her a bad dog. Then I felt awful about it. Because she was the best dog in the world.

So I carried Sugar downstairs to give her a peace offering of cheddar cheese, and then I decided to take her for a walk. But before I grabbed her leash and said the magic four-letter word that would send her into absolute pandemonium, I gargled with some minty mouthwash and took my blond hair down. Then I changed into a push-up bra, put on some ripped jeans and boots, and reapplied my makeup with extra layers of lip gloss.

I lived on a street with an unlimited supply of cute boys, and even though I had a boyfriend at the time, I still flirted my teenage heart out whenever possible. I had to be prepared for an interaction with the opposite sex at all times. Attention made me feel I mattered. One look from a boy said, *I see you. You're important. I want you.* And when you're sixteen and your daddy's toe-tapping passion for life and music and even you, his daughter, has vanished, you can't be wanted enough.

Since it was freezing outside, I threw on a jacket but kept it unzipped so that my cleavage was still visible. I clasped the metal end of Sugar's leash to her pink collar and she whirled around herself in excitement, tangling herself in her leash. Her butt wiggled along with her tail as we stepped out the front door.

The snow on the ground was dirty and half-melted, but Sugar found a relatively clean pile that looked like a mound of mashed potatoes in our driveway. She looked back at me as if to say, *"Look at this glorious pile of fluff!"* before she flung herself into it. Then she rolled around and made doggy snow angels. I wrapped my arms around myself to keep warm, staring up at a crescent moon behind a cluster of silver clouds. Icicles hung from bare branches all around us, and snow melted from tall roofs pointing to a starry sky.

After Sugar slurped up some snow like ice cream, we walked under the faint yellow light of streetlamps through our small neighborhood filled with New England–style homes. Many were decorated with Christmas lights, flowerpots and rocking chairs on the front porches, and chandeliers in the front windows.

I could see my breath between my lips, and every time we passed by a cute boy's house, my heart pounded so fast there was barely any space between beats. In the hush of night I could hear that pounding, loud girl cries from deep in my chest. I looked around with the alertness of a prey animal for a boy to be shoveling snow, smoking a cigarette, parking a car, even turning the light on in a bedroom window.

Part of that was me being a giddy, horny teenager, but another part of it was pure desperation. At 9 P.M. on a Wednesday, I was intentionally freezing my ass off, with so many rips in my jeans I might as well have been wearing shorts, and showing enough cleavage to become the main attraction in a rap video that already had a truckload of cleavage in it. I had enough makeup on to compete with a drag queen—wanting so badly for somebody, anybody, to call me beautiful.

While I waited to be seen and worried about my hair frizzing, Sugar pranced alongside me with no concern for formalities or politeness, no taming of joy or wildness, no self-consciousness.

Maybe all along, Sugar messed with my makeup bag on purpose. Maybe my sweet dog was trying to tell me over and over again: *Stop your futile efforts to be seen. There is nothing you could ever do to make you unlovable.*

4

S OON AFTER I embarked on my makeover kick, I broke
up with my boyfriend, Tyler, whom I'd been dating for
nine months. He was a year older than I was and played
for our school's golf and basketball teams. I made signs for him
at his games, and we went to the prom together, where it never
even occurred to us to have sex later or get wasted. Our favorite activity was playing the stop sign game. We'd put the car in
park at every stop sign we came to and make out until someone
behind us honked. This was the height of our rebellion.

But thanks to my new, tight clothes and makeup, more guys
began to notice me. It wasn't long before I thought Tyler, as
well as the stop sign game, was sort of boring, and I ended it.

Soon enough, I found myself talking to a twenty-two-year-
old guy with spiky hair who went to community college but
for some reason was at a high school house party. I didn't find
him sketchy. I found him hot and mysterious and mature. He
grabbed my hand and said that he wanted to show me his "fucking crazy" car, which was a hideous mint color and parked on
a side street where there weren't many lights. After we finished
our foamy beers in plastic red cups, we tossed them in someone's yard, and he laid me down on the warm hood.

He nibbled on my ear a little, then took off my shirt and

leopard-print bra and dug his tongue into my mouth. His tongue ring felt strange, almost like a loose tooth, and after a few slobbery minutes of kissing, his tongue moved inside of my ear, then grazed down my neck, then lingered around my breasts, then moved inside of my belly button, which I'd recently pierced. He grabbed on to the sides of my stomach, my love handles, and pinched them hard. Unlike Tyler, who lovingly wrapped his arms around me, this kid grabbed my ass. He bit my lips. He pinched my flesh, calling me "fucking sexy" and "fucking hot." I clenched my eyes shut in self-consciousness and gripped his T-shirt at the center of his back.

I didn't feel sexy or hot. What I felt, especially when he pinched my love handles, was fat. A feeling I'd never consciously experienced before.

Countless doctors would later stare at me behind their thick glasses and wrinkly foreheads and pretend smiles and eyes that thought they knew everything and tell me that I was wrong. "Fat is not a feeling," they'd say.

But they didn't know what it was like to be half-naked on the hood of a mint-green car with a boy whose name you didn't even know, whose life you didn't even know, who in some vague and all-consuming way makes you feel unworthy of him.

They didn't know how effective it was to pin all of your pain on a body part. To blame the shape of your life on the shape of your body. To find pain delicious.

They didn't know what it was like to wrap your skinny, shaved legs around an untouchable boy, and to pray to him with your lips.

They didn't know what it was like to feel like the girl standing next to you has a body glowing in neon colors, and you're just a gritty speck of black chalk.

They didn't know what it was like to feel fat.

·   ·   ·

THE DAY AFTER the mint-green-car make-out session, I decided that it was time to lose weight. The era of bootylicious Beyoncé had just begun, and even though I'd heard that men liked something to hold on to, I was not immune to the bombardment of messages on infallibility, thinness, and perfection inside every nook and cranny of teenage existence.

Some part of me must have known that toned stomachs and Kardashian asses and designer wardrobes could never compete with the beauty of the human heart, but where was that wisdom when I needed it the most? Not on MTV. Not in the hallways of my high school. Not in *Seventeen* magazine. And not anywhere easily accessible within me.

In my mind, looking good had quickly become just as important, if not more important, than living well. The rap lyrics I memorized talked about *getting mine* and *going hard* and *making it*. Nobody was talking about *giving love* and *going easy* and *seeing how we'd already made it*. Nobody was singing about how when we die, all that will have mattered is how we felt in our lives, not how we looked or who we impressed. And unless I was watching a Lifetime movie, nobody died. Maybe they died in Africa or in nursing homes, but that wasn't where I lived. I lived within the sheltered walls of a suburban, mostly white high school, and death was just a concept to me. There was all the time in the world to kill staring at my tiny cell phone screen, waiting for a text or a ring. Waiting to feel alive. Waiting to matter.

This was the time before Instagram and filters and profile pictures, but even then, a photograph of the moment seemed far more important than how I felt in the moment itself. And I didn't think my love handles would photograph well.

So I went on my first diet. It was a terrible diet, but I didn't know that yet because I'd never paid attention to what I ate or to what the magazines and books and celebrities and doctors said about eating. I was positive liquids couldn't be fattening. There was nothing to them, right? No substance. So I allowed myself to eat one bagel in the morning and then nothing else until after school, when I had a Venti Caramel Macchiato Frappuccino from Starbucks. My favorite part was the whipped cream with the caramel syrup drizzled on top, which I scooped out and licked off my fingers.

I can't tell you how much I looked forward to that caramel syrup drizzle, my hard-earned, sweet reward for starving myself throughout the day. After a lifetime of loving food and loving to eat and never thinking too much about what I ate, restricting myself was a very difficult thing to do. I mean, my first words after *Dada* and *Mama* were *bobble* and *cracker*. In most baby pictures, my face is covered with frosting or spaghetti sauce.

Dieting for me was impossibly hard, like jumping into a triathlon without any preparation. During meals, it became tough to carry on a conversation with anyone for very long. I was distracted by how much my mother ate and my sister ate and that stranger over there ate, and all the food I pushed around my plate but refused to lift to my mouth. Dinner plates no longer contained food, but flashing red lights, and if a chocolate cake was in the room, I lusted over it like a teenybopper over One Direction.

Yet after about a month on my rigorous diet, and all the sacrifice it required, I still hadn't lost any weight. Then I read in a magazine that bagels were bad, and Frappuccinos were really, really bad, the caloric equivalent of a Big Mac. I buried my face into my hands and growled into my palms, feeling so ridiculously stupid and pissed about my wasted efforts that I almost cried. But then a familiar voice, louder than any kindness or compassion I could generate for myself, said not to cry. It disguised its unmerciful beat-downs as pep talks and said to get my shit together and do better.

I tossed the magazine in the trash and decided that I was never getting anything but black coffee with skim milk at Starbucks. I promised myself that I'd only eat salad for dinner that night, and then I'd go online and research how to do this dieting thing right.

But dinner was Mom's delicious broccoli and cheese casserole—creamy with bits of bright orange cheddar cheese bubbling on top. As I shoveled the first bite into my mouth, the heaviness and flavor were nearly orgasmic. And before I knew it, I was heaping seconds and thirds onto my plate.

Dad was off somewhere drinking, probably near his health club, and as usual, none of us talked about it. A vase of limp, red roses sat on the table, flowers he bought Mom after his last bender. ("I don't want any more flowers!" she screamed. "I want you to stop lying to me!")

Julie pushed the flowers aside to get to the casserole. She was three years younger than I was and ever since she came into the world fourteen years earlier, we'd been inseparable. As kids, we swam in our self-made sisterworld. We felt things we didn't yet have names for, and we felt them together. Even though we both had rooms of our own growing up, we preferred to sleep side by side, surrounded by stuffed animals. In elementary school, we shared the same seat on the school bus and sometimes held hands. On all three occasions that somebody made fun of our close bond, I smacked them—and once with a heavy book.

I'd always seen myself as her protector, and perhaps that's why, when Julie began to shift from the little girl I knew who loved to draw and dance to a teenager full of angst and rage,

I couldn't shake the feeling that her angst and rage was my fault. By fourteen, Julie had not yet discovered black eyeliner and emo music—she had not yet discovered all the ways she wanted to escape her own life—but I could feel something heavy pressing up against her chest as if it were my own chest, something boiling in her heart as if it were my own.

Tonight, she fought with Mom about not wanting to go to high school, an argument that continued for the next four years, basically until the day she graduated, when Mom and I cheered in the audience as she crossed the stage with her diploma. Dad wept, drunk out of his mind.

"I want to be an artist!" Julie bellowed across the table. "I want to draw."

She clenched her fork and sighed a heavy breath. Then she looked over at me to come to her defense, but I just shrugged my shoulders and kept eating. Julie's hating school and my loving school was just one of the many differences between us. I was an easy baby who ate everything, rarely cried, and slept twelve hours a night, even once through a hurricane. Mom says that Julie didn't sleep for the first two years of her life, cried whenever anyone but my parents or me held her, and pinched her mouth shut no matter how many airplanes Mom made with her baby food. We looked physically different, too, enough for people to question if we were even sisters. Going into her freshman year, Julie's hair was naturally dark brown (though she'd soon start to highlight it with hues of red and purple), while mine was shades lighter, and I was five eight and she was five one.

But we had the same color eyes, blue like our mother's. And being Julie's big sister was how I defined myself first. And then I was other things. An animal lover. A dancer. A pimply horse.

"It's not up for discussion," Mom said to Julie, her eyes

burning with annoyance. "You're finishing high school. You have no choice."

Meanwhile, I ate until the waistband of my jeans dug into my skin and it hurt to breathe. Every moment that the cheesy fattening badness remained in my stomach was another moment that took me farther away from being like the girls in *Shape* magazine. But still, I couldn't stop.

I remembered Amber, a perfect, brown-eyed popular girl at school. She looked like a blond version of Angelina Jolie. Her hips were surely a size zero. Her hair hung down her back, so smooth it shimmered under the bright lights of our high school's hallways. She had a sweet delicate voice, and she was always the prettiest girl in the room.

The other day, Amber had told me about how she stuck a spoon in her mouth to make herself vomit. Her eyes got wider and brighter, almost dilated when she said, "It's the best feeling. You feel, like, so empty."

I excused myself from the dinner table. Mom and Julie barely noticed because they were still fighting. I went upstairs and locked the door to the bathroom that my sister and I shared, where we blared hip-hop and sang into our hairbrushes, where we bathed Sugar with peppermint-scented soap. The walls were pale blue, with a painting of a little girl splashing in a big bucket near the toilet. I turned on the shower and then cursed myself for forgetting a spoon. I'd have to use my fingers.

As I pulled my hair back, I thought about kneeling down, but then I decided to just try it standing. I leaned over the toilet and hesitantly put two fingers in my mouth. My plan was to sort of flick the soft ball hanging at the back of my throat, like a strep test. I tried it once and gagged.

That coughing sound and the jerk of my body startled me. I looked down at my stomach pushing taut against my skin. At the thought of how much food I ate, I got onto my knees. I unbuttoned my jeans so I could breathe easier. Then I pinched my fingers together and shoved them in my mouth as fast and forceful as a punch. Vomit came pouring out, still warm and salty. My stomach churned. My eyes watered. My nails scraped against the roof of my mouth. I jabbed at the back of my throat again and again until acid burned up it and felt like hell coming out between my chapped lips.

When nothing was left, I sat back on my heels, wiped my mouth with the back of my wrist, and then flushed. I washed my hands in my sister's sink, turning the water as hot as it could go, as if to sanitize my fingers the way you might a baking dish.

I was disgusted with myself and vowed never to do this again, but then I lifted my head and noticed my reflection. Instead of seeing bloodshot eyes and a lack of color in my skin, I experienced the strangest sensation. In the mirror, a thinner girl stared back at me. Her face had lost its round shape, and her cheeks were more pronounced, and I could see her collarbone, too. I stared at her in shock. She almost looked like a model.

Then, she spoke. She looked into my sunken eyes and whispered that I could throw up more than food. I could throw up my problems. I could throw up my love handles and frizzy hair and acne. I could throw up my B-plus average and missing my dad like crazy and the rage that never escaped my mouth.

I could throw up the difference between the girl I was and the girl I believed I was supposed to be.

5

BY THE TIME high school came to an end, I was puking three to four times a week and working out every day. I dropped from a size four to a size zero and reveled in the praise and respect people gave me. They had all these questions, like I was some kind of weight loss guru. *Do you eat cheese? How often do you work out? Is it running? Is it yoga?*

What's your secret? they'd ask.

I'd smile, drinking in their approval, and pretend like my appearance happened naturally. What would they have said if I actually told them about the toilet and the vomit? And what if I knew where this all would inevitably take me?

Even if someone had carefully explained to me that I was trading the poetry of my soul for a sad language of numbers— pant sizes, scale readings, calorie charts—I doubt I would have listened.

EVERY DAY, I abided by a diet of salad, fruit, and coffee. My mind was black-and-white, all-or-nothing. There were good foods (nonfat, low cal) and there were bad foods (sugary, fattening, caloric). My rigid goal every day was to eat only good foods, and when I didn't, I felt morbidly ashamed.

I usually starved until midnight or 1 A.M., when my family was asleep and I couldn't take the hunger pains anymore. I'd sneak down into the kitchen and take a bite of something healthy, like a granola bar, and then another bite, and then another. The more bites I took, the further I felt driven toward the edge of a cliff. There came a point when I was holding on for dear life to my perfect diet. Holding on by just a few fingers.

Then I would let go. My teeth crunched down hard on candy and chips and cookies, all the food I wouldn't dream of touching during the day. Sugar usually sat on the tile floor with her head cocked, alert to the sounds of containers and bags opening and closing, waiting for potential crumb droppings.

Sometimes I cried while I binged. Sometimes I thought and felt nothing. Rarely did I look down at Sugar, and always, I prayed that no one would wake up and catch me. My hands were usually covered in peanut butter or the cold pasta salad I dug my fingers into. There was no time for forks or plates or drinks between bites. There was only the desire to fill up, followed immediately by an urgent need to get empty.

Something beyond my physical body was ravenous. I hungered not to feel that something anymore. I craved a lucid, single-minded state. With the sensation of food sliding down my throat, my mouth constantly moving, my belly growing fuller and tighter by the second, I'd soon forget I had a care in the world.

When I left the kitchen to throw up in the downstairs bathroom, Sugar usually continued to lick the crumbs off the floor. Then I carried her upstairs to my room and we climbed into bed under dozens of glow-in-the-dark stars and planets stuck to my ceiling. I lifted the covers so that Sugar could snuggle close to me—her twenty-pound body under my pink sheets and blankets, her head facing me and sharing my pillow.

With our noses just a few inches apart, she curled all four of her legs into my chest and stomach, and I placed my head on top of hers, stroking her soft ears until I fell asleep.

Throughout the night, she never pushed me to the edge of the bed. Sugar would steal my sandwich in a heartbeat but not an inch of the space where I rested my head. I always found that remarkable.

We often woke up in the same position as when we fell asleep, and I envied that each day, she woke up happy, with no stories of yesterday on her mind. Sometimes it was like she was the only sanity left in that big gray house, her bright eyes whispering, *But the sun came up again. But this moment is brand-new.*

In the mornings, she often copied me like a game of Simon Says. When I sighed, her ears twitched. When I stretched, she stretched out all of her limbs at once, and her warm body stiffened and relaxed against mine. Sometimes when I yawned, she did, too, sticking out and curling her pink tongue. She always wanted to stay in bed for as long as possible. If I made the slightest motion that signified I might be getting up, she climbed up onto my chest and did downward dog, then curled up nose to tail so as to make sure I wasn't going anywhere.

6

LONG BEFORE THE magical day my parents deemed my sister and me old enough to take a care of a dog, I knew that her name would be Sugar. I had developed an unhealthy and slightly obsessive relationship with the ingredient at a young age—sneaking in an extra cupcake or two or five at birthday parties—but this wasn't the reason.

The reason was that my grandma Elsie used the word *sugar* all the time, and I adored my grandma. I still do. She's eighty-seven now and dating a man in his sixties who has trouble keeping up with Grandma's busy schedule of bowling, swimming, poker playing, and most of all, dancing.

When I was younger, Grandma used to grab me and cover my face with hot pink lipstick prints, squealing all the while: "Oh honey, gimme some sugar!" She'd kiss me like she wanted to eat me alive and say again and again, "Oh, c'mon, just a little more sugar!"

So at an early age, Grandma taught me that "sugar" meant a crazy, almost reckless amount of love. A love that couldn't be contained or restrained. A love that was silly, ridiculous, loud, and all-consuming.

I couldn't imagine a better name for my first dog.

· · ·

WHEN I WAS nine, and Julie was six, we finally welcomed the dog we'd been dreaming of into our family. Sugar was eight weeks old, a mere three pounds, and only slightly taller than the grass in our front yard. Her white fur was so silky soft, and her body was so delicate. She had bubble-gum pink paws, long, humanlike eyelashes, and the most expressive, bright black eyes.

From the very start, Julie and I treated Sugar more like a princess and a human sister than a dog. Once the neighbors called to report that it was pouring rain, and Julie (age seven) was walking down the road, sopping wet, holding the umbrella over Sugar. We routinely dressed her up in doll clothes and paraded her around in a red wagon. We snapped pictures of her like paparazzi and kissed her at least fifty times a day. She not only tolerated our relentless doting on her—she pined for it.

Tiny as she was, Sugar did everything big. She never just gave one kiss, always ten or so at a time. She gobbled up her food and treats in seconds. She gnawed on her bones until they were gone. She ran so fast that sometimes she'd tumble into a series of somersaults, but then just keep on running. She squeaked her squeaky toys until they squeaked no more.

She also didn't have a stop button when it came to cuddling, and she preferred a human lap to a dog bed any day of the week. She slept with my parents most of the time, but on the nights Julie and I were upset, she came to sleep with us, as though she sensed our pain and made a conscious choice to be with whoever most needed comfort.

That's not to say that Sugar never upset us herself. In fact, sometimes she drove me to the point of hysterics. Her insatiable appetite caused us to bring her to the vet at least a half a dozen times during just the first two years of her life. She pulled the dining room tablecloth down and ate forty peanut butter cookies with Hershey's kisses in them. She moved a mini-refrigerator in our garage to get at a block of mouse poisoning (we found her swaying like she was on drugs, with blue powder on her muzzle). She ate French "bonbons," the foil wrappers included. Once, she slurped up a half-dead bee off the ground. The bee's wings may not have worked, but his stinger still did, and he stung Sugar in the throat. It caused an allergic reaction and instant swelling.

After each digestive-related crisis, I wound up in the backseat of the minivan with Sugar in my lap, Julie beside me, Mom running stop signs on the way to the vet. I was always the hysterical one, hyperventilating and wailing during the whole drive. "Sugar's going to die, she's going to die!"

My baby sister was always more composed. Mom recalls once looking in the van rearview mirror to see Julie punching me in the arm and saying in the toughest voice a six-year-old could muster, "Shannon! Get it together, Sugar's not going to die!"

MY SISTER WAS the most adorable child on the planet. You may think I'm biased, but I'm telling you. Julie. Was. Adorable.

As a kid, she was always the shortest and most petite one in her class. She had bright blue eyes that popped against her brown ringlets of curls, her ridiculous dimples, and her tendency to mix her words up (she had trouble remembering that her first-grade teacher was Ms. Berger and not Mrs. Cheeseburger).

By the time she was fifteen, she was still adorable to me. Still young. And still trying to knock some sense into her big sister.

As far as I knew, she was still drawing cartoons and practicing dance moves to Destiny's Child in her bedroom at night. I had no idea that she was crying in bed about my eating disorder. Maybe I just didn't want to let myself know.

One night, a few weeks before I left for college, she crammed her tiny body into the cabinets beneath the double sinks in our shared bathroom. She must have pushed through an abyss of tampons, body lotion, and nail polish to pretzel herself inside that cabinet, waiting for me to come up the stairs.

Sometime around 11 P.M., after I'd finished my fifth bowl of sugar-drenched Cheerios, I flung open the bathroom door and turned on the bath faucet to cover up the sound of my puking. Then I leaned over the toilet with my hand in my mouth.

Julie busted out of the cupboards with shampoo bottles rolling after her.

"Stop it!" she yelled.

My knees fell to the white tile floor and I choked on my own breath. I wiped my slimy fingers and knuckles on my jeans as Julie stood over me in her hot pink pajamas. Her eyes brimmed with tears. "You said you'd never lie to me," she said.

This was true. Years earlier, we had crossed our hearts and hoped to die that the world could lie to us and our parents could lie to us, but we would never lie to each other. Because we were sisters. Because it was just the two of us. Because we only had each other.

I took a deep breath and flushed the toilet then turned the tub faucet off.

The drain sucked up the remains of cold water, and I told Julie I never lied to her. I just didn't want her to know. I didn't want to worry her.

"I'm sorry, I'll stop," I said, my eyes cast down.

"You're lying again," she said.

Then she turned around and slammed the bathroom door. I

followed her to her bedroom down the hall, but it was locked. I knocked and started pounding on the door so hard that my palms stung.

Mom came out of her bedroom, her hair all disheveled. She wore a Providence College T-shirt; I would begin classes there soon. Mom had worked a ten-hour day and looked beyond tired, beyond done, beyond pissed.

"What's going on?" she said.

"Nothing, Mom. Everything's fine," I said.

"Liar!" Julie shrieked from behind her bedroom door.

Sugar slept with Julie that night.

7

A T PROVIDENCE COLLEGE, a world filled with green manicured lawns, tall brick buildings, and preppy kids who liked to party, things seemed to get better.

I made a close group of girlfriends with whom I did just about everything. We traveled to the Bahamas and Jamaica and Vegas. We piled into sketchy bars and clubs with fake IDs, all of us "twenty-two" and from "Vermont." We ran side by side on treadmills at Gold's Gym and across the quad drunk and topless after finals. We studied in each other's rooms while jacked up on Diet Coke and sugar-free Swedish Fish. We shopped for outfits for Halloween parties, toga parties, Mardi Gras parties, formal parties, St. Patrick's Day parties, eighties parties, and lots of themed parties that ended with the word *hoes* (CEOs and Office Hoes; Golf Pros and Tennis Hoes, et cetera).

We shook salt on our wrists, licked, and downed tequila. We spent our money on fat-free fro-yo, Coach wristlets, Tiffany jewelry, and insanely expensive pieces of cloth and ripped denim from Abercrombie & Fitch. We danced (and occasionally fell) on beer-soaked floors, and we ate lots of late-night, undercooked, overpriced food at Golden Crust Pizza.

We took selfies before selfies were a thing. We posted pictures on Shutterfly before Facebook was a phenomenon. And we ate almost all our meals together, which lessened my bulimic episodes to about once or twice a month.

I was an English major with unrealistic ideas about writing and hopes of someday becoming the next Carrie Bradshaw of *Sex and the City* (she was more than a fictional character to me). I also had a slight obsession with Toni Morrison, whose books I read and reread, discovering something new about the human heart every time. I printed out Toni Morrison quotes and taped them to my closet doors and my wooden desk back at home in Connecticut. One of my favorite quotes: "If there's a book you really want to read, but it hasn't been written yet, then you must write it."

That's exactly what Toni Morrison did at the age of thirty-nine, as a single mother of two, when she wrote her first novel, *The Bluest Eye*. Morrison didn't do what I often did, letting my mind convince me that I was too fill-in-the-blank-with-something-belittling to accomplish my goals. Instead, she went for it, and she accomplished nothing less than the Pulitzer and the Nobel Prize.

ON THE WEEKENDS, usually hungover, I volunteered for the nonprofit organization Big Brothers Big Sisters, where I mentored a fourteen-year-old girl named Joyce who faced so many unthinkable atrocities by the age of ten—rape, her cousin being shot on his front porch, a father in prison—that I had no idea how she was still standing. Joyce was a few inches shorter than me with dark skin, black frizzy hair, which she sometimes dyed blue, and a mind filled with poetry. She only cried when it was raining outside, she once told me, because the rain made her feel less alone.

I admired Joyce for turning to the rain in her loneliness. It reminded me how one day, Julie, who was crying about our dad being in jail, stopped midsentence and stared out at the ocean. We were walking on a mostly deserted beach in California, when all of a sudden she ran toward the water with her clothes on and dove headfirst into the froth. A few seconds later, she stood up and turned to me in waist-high water, her hair soaked, her mouth grinning, her whole demeanor changed to something brighter.

I wished that I turned to rain, or to the ocean, to help me when I felt sad or alone. I hated that there were still some nights I turned to food for comfort.

As my friends got into relationships with men throughout college, I sacrificed true intimacy for fleeting feelings of fullness and emptiness. I didn't have sex with the guys who occupied my bed, but I rarely went to bed alone. Sometimes I liked the person on the pillow beside me, but more often he was there because I didn't want to be by myself. That's when I got depressed. That's when I was most likely to binge and purge. That's when my primary relationship took over, which was still sick and abusive and with food. No man could compete with it.

Some nights, I stuffed myself so full it felt like a boulder was inside me. Then I threw up. I released the boulder. For a moment I felt orgasmically empty. Empty and alone.

Hunched over the toilet, my stomach still in spasms from retching, I let myself drift into the lightness of my body, the sweet hollowness of silence. But in the short walk from the bathroom to my bedroom, that sweetness dissolved. When I flung myself onto my dorm mattress, I felt an aching that did not seem to belong in a space shared by four party girls with flowery bedspreads. Just beneath a Dave Matthews poster across the room, a screen saver flashed the words "Live, Love, Laugh," mocking the burning in my throat and the weight in my bones.

• • •

EVENTUALLY I FOUND a therapist, a tall and thin lady with long brown hair and a soothing voice that seemed meant for guided meditation tapes. I saw Dr. Cameron once a week for four years, beginning my freshman year. In her tiny nook of an office across campus, everything she said was spot-on. Unlike the first therapist I saw, an old, cranky bastard who told me to simply drink water when I felt the urge to binge, Dr. Cameron told me to breathe. She told me to do whatever I could to slow down the body and the mind when it came to food. She talked about bulimia as an illness, an addiction, a serious and fatal disease. She seemed to understand that food, like an invisible lasso, pulled me away from the places my soul wanted to be: taking a walk outside, dancing with my sister, reading a book.

I would leave Dr. Cameron's office knowing with every ounce of my being that this stuff had to stop. I had to change. Slow down. Breathe. Take better care of myself.

Sometimes I felt so inspired after meeting with her that I read Rumi on the quad for an hour. Or I took a dance or a yoga class. Or I picked up Joyce and we went to the mall. Or I called Julie to tell her how much I loved and missed her.

But sometimes I found myself in the student cafeteria inhaling food as though I hadn't eaten a meal in days. Which was sometimes literally the case.

How quickly I forgot everything I felt so sure of in Dr. Cameron's office! Therapy amnesia, I called it. Sometimes I found it funny that everything I worked so hard to know and understand in therapy or yoga or books shot out of me like a cannonball in the moments I needed it most. But most of the time, it scared me and served as further proof that when the shit hit the fan, I couldn't count on myself. I was a runner, and often to places that only made my hurt worse in the end.

Dr. Cameron told me again and again how shame poisoned and destroyed a life. Her message was always the same, and it echoed everything my mother had ever taught me: the most important thing in the world is not how you look but how you feel. Success isn't determined by what you do for a living but by the extent to which you learn how to mother yourself, to regard your fragile and temporary being with love.

Mom used to always say, "Be good to you."

This meant embrace with both hands the good things this world offered, to do the things that would bring joy and health rather than pain and misery. Even the trees did it, Mom said. They never refused the rain or sunshine they needed to grow and thrive. They soaked it up, deep down into their roots. It was my job to do the same.

I heard my mother. And I heard Dr. Cameron. But I heard the voices in my own mind louder: Lose. Weight. And. Everything. Will. Be. Fine.

8

SUGAR WAS A spoiled and prissy dog, but she loved to get good and dirty, too. Whenever I came home on college breaks and it was nice outside, I brought her to a nearby park with a handful of paths in the woods. Sugar stopped to smell the roses and the urine and the piles of horseshit, of course, but her steadfast desire was always to move deeper and deeper into the forest, as if every step nourished another inch of her canine soul.

Celebration was continually on Sugar's brain but especially so in the outdoors. She'd get this wolfish expression on her face, and her nostrils moved nonstop in total rapture of the earthly scents all around her. She became so wild-hearted and happy, rejoicing in every creature she halfheartedly chased, in every leafless branch she bit between her teeth, in every new scent she tracked. When squirrels ran up the trunks of trees, she made an admirable but hopeless attempt to climb after them. When birds opened their throats to sing above us, Sugar paused and looked up, listening with perked ears. Sometimes she stood and balanced on her hind legs as if trying to see or hear them better.

If Sugar encountered a feather of any sort, she lost all control. She'd pick it up and shake it in her mouth like a dead animal, and then run around in figure eights like her butt was on fire. If I tossed the feather in the air and the wind carried it, she leapt three or four feet off the ground to snatch it, her little legs kicking when she jumped. I'd laugh so hard that sometimes it felt like there were three of us there: me, my dog, and my laughter echoing through the woods.

No matter what kind of day it was, Sugar's love for life reminded me of my own reasons for loving life: the stones glistening beneath my feet, black wings flying overhead, leaves trembling on branches, a stretch of pink sky. To be with Sugar was to know that at any moment, I too could celebrate nature simply because it was there. I too could be wild-hearted and happy.

The paths were never crowded or busy—sometimes we went on two-hour walks without encountering another person. How good it felt to be in the quiet. How good it felt to wash off my makeup and throw on a T-shirt and get some dirt under my fingernails. How good it felt to move my body on something other than a treadmill. Most of all, how good it felt to be with a little dog whose zest for living was bigger than life itself.

During the rare times we did come across another person and/or dog, Sugar pulled at the end of the leash to make the meeting happen sooner. All her life, she was eager to greet dogs, cats, horses, and people of all sorts. In Sugar's eyes, everybody was interesting, everybody was worth a good sniff.

When Sugar got older and couldn't walk as far, we'd sit under the shade of an oak tree. I'd toss acorns at the sky or stroke Sugar's back, even if it was covered in mud. Bugs crawled on my jeans while Sugar's white, bushy tail thumped on the grass beside me. And from that quiet place, I could see beyond myself and self-made troubles. The music of my mind changed from heavy metal to something sweeter. Or maybe it just came into tune. Everything in view multiplied, the sprouting weeds and wildflowers, the blades of grass, the birds, the flies. A snake could slither by, and I wouldn't feel the need to run. Mosquitoes could land on my arms and poke their straws into my skin, but I wouldn't want to swat them dead.

Gazing out into the forest, I didn't want to run from or hurt anybody, not even myself. I just wanted to sit under a canopy of green with my sweet dog by my side, who sometimes lay down and fell into a light sleep. *(Was she dreaming of chasing rabbits? Or were her dreams more complex and surprising than that?)* Or she played with my shoelaces like she did when she was a puppy. Or she dug a hole, stopping every now and then to turn her head and press her ear to the earth, as if listening to secrets from belowground.

Sometimes I could almost hear them, too, whispers of abundance and rejuvenation.

9

MY JUNIOR OF year of college, French language CDs and headphones became as necessary as a leash on my walks to the park with Sugar, since I had been accepted to study abroad for my spring semester at the Collège International de Cannes. Every day leading up to the big trip overseas, I practiced the language and imagined myself taking delicate bites of a Nutella crêpe at a neighborhood *boulangerie,* or sipping Provençal wine on a waterfront terrace, or French-kissing some dark-haired European under the Eiffel Tower. Cannes had become my promised land, the place where I'd free myself from my gluttonous relationship with food once and for all, and learn how to eat with all the tasteful restraint of a Frenchwoman. My departure date to the French Riviera couldn't come soon enough.

But on the morning I was supposed to fly out to Europe, I looked through my bedroom window and the world had gone colorless. White dust poured from the sky and had already piled a foot high on the ground. I turned on the TV and the weatherman was all jacked up because there were 50 mph winds, drifts up to three feet high in some towns, and piles of snow on the road as high as mailboxes. Boston's Logan International Airport, where I was supposed to fly out of, was shut down.

I went downstairs to the kitchen and found a note written on a napkin from my mother, "Went to check on Dad. Be back."

They had recently separated, and Dad was now living in an apartment complex called "The Mansions" fifteen minutes away, though *living* probably isn't the correct term. More accurately, he was drinking himself to death there, drinking until someone found him unconscious and called 911. This morning, that person was my mother, who found him facedown on the floor in his underwear surrounded by empty vodka and Bacardi bottles. While he was rushed to the hospital and put on suicide watch, I spent an hour on the phone trying to find a way to get out of the country through JFK International.

ONCE I FINALLY transferred flights for later that afternoon out of New York, I put on my gloves, boots, and a jacket over my pajamas to let Sugar outside. She paused on the front steps of the porch and stared up at the sky as if to formally thank the clouds that had so kindly poured out such a fun playscape for her that morning. Then she dove into a thick sheet of white, sinking down to her chest. The snow camouflaged her well. If she stood still, all I could see was a black nose and two button eyes staring back at me.

There wasn't a slice of blue in the sky, just one gray cloud rolling into another. The wind swirled and howled through bare trees—breaking branches, relocating flower bushes, and surely messing up more than a few animal homes out in the woods. I cupped snow in my gloves and clumped it into a ball, then threw it high in the air. Sugar chased the ball, then manically dug into the snow wherever it landed. A flurry of white shot out from behind her busy paws, and I couldn't help but laugh every time. She was like a mini-snowblower.

When Mom came home a half hour later, I held Sugar in a towel by the fireplace. She was shivering cold and absolutely delighted with herself, but when Mom entered the room, her tail stopped swishing back and forth.

Mom paced the room and reeled about my father; she still in crisis mode and running on adrenaline after rescuing Dad once again. Mom said that the roads were a nightmare, but for the next hour, she called a dozen bus and taxi companies, none of which were operating due to the weather. The only form of transportation she could find to get us to JFK was a limo service, and she booked it.

"You're not missing a minute of your dream," she said, pulling out her credit card.

So that afternoon in the thick of the storm, Mom and I climbed into the back of a black stretch limo. We reclined on heated leather seats, sipped on sparkling water, and switched the radio to a station playing Alicia Keys. Mom said she didn't know what happened to the man she married. He was a ghost to her now. She said that she was sorry I didn't have a dad in my life anymore, and I told her not to apologize for him. I looked out the window at the empty roads and darkening sky. There was a purple hue to the snow, and the flakes had turned icy, banging against the glass with every strong gust of wind.

A stark loneliness and harshness filled the world outside, a world that part of me was thrilled to leave for the next five months. But another part of me felt guilty. I would be the first of my family to visit Europe, and sitting beside Mom, it felt like an opportunity I didn't deserve. If anyone deserved it, it was her . . . working long hours since Dad had lost his job, fighting for my sister to not drop out of high school, and worrying about me. My weight had stabilized, but she sensed that something was still wrong. Whenever she asked me about my life or about my weight, she never got the whole story. What I shrugged off as "eating issues" were the symptom of a deeper problem: an inability to be honest with myself and the people who loved me. A refusal to admit my need for help.

When we arrived at JFK, I stepped out of the car and into a foot-high pile of snow. The wetness seeped into the wool of my Ugg boots, soaking the tips of my socks, numbing my toes. While the limo driver pulled out my two enormous bags from the trunk, Mom stood with me on the curb wearing a heavy red jacket. Her cheeks were rosy pink and her eyes were glassy. She hugged me harder and longer than I can ever remember being hugged.

Then she said, "Sweetheart, promise me that you'll be good to you."

She said it with desperation this time. Not a request, but a plea.

AT THE COLLÈGE International de Cannes, I walked around more or less stunned for about two days. The school was essentially three white buildings with peach cobblestone roofs in a U-shape, directly facing the Mediterranean Sea. Inside, entire floors were bright orange, strawberry pink, and lemon yellow, making the place feel like a fruity funhouse. In addition to classrooms and student housing, there was a theater, a gym, a library, a phone room with yellow booths that looked straight out of the eighties, basketball and volleyball courts, and best of all, a sundeck with white lawn chairs facing the ocean.

There were about fifty students from the States, and others from Europe, South Africa, and Asia. We finished up classes every weekday around noon and spent the rest of the day tanning on the beach, where the waves were so gentle you could float on your back and be rocked to sleep. Cruise ships floated near a red and white lighthouse in the distance. Le Vieux Port was just to the left of us, where fishing boats and sailboats lived out their lives on the water, right beside million-dollar yachts.

Every day, young men whistled and gawked shamelessly at the women walking past. Old men played volleyball for hours in purple and lime-green speedos. Children ran around naked, slurping melted ice cream and sand into their mouths. Labrador retrievers leapt into the air to catch tennis balls on the beach next to Yorkies who could barely get their legs off the ground. Miniature poodles and French bulldogs sat next to their owners at beach cafés. Stray cats hid behind mopeds and tiny cars—once I even found ten of them in a back alley, a feline hangout spot, it seemed, after a long day scrounging for baguette crumbs and mice and water.

The ocean wasn't warm like a bath but not ice-cube cold, either—somewhere perfectly in between. A collection of gray and blue rocks was scattered along the shoreline, but there were also some maroon rocks that looked like little hearts, as if someone had painted and sculpted them by hand.

And yes, indeed, everybody was topless on the beach: old ladies with white hair and saggy boobs; large women with big breasts; beautiful girls; young students. I nearly fell over at the sight of so many naked chests, as did most of the American students of the male sex. Despite my Hippodrome dance years earlier, I had no plans of sprawling out on the beach like that now, sober and in broad daylight.

But eventually, two months into the semester, I did. My hands made the decision to do it, reaching under my hair to untie the knot around my neck, unclipping the back of my top, and tossing it into the creamy sand.

I got up and walked past the men and women swimming in

paint buckets of golden-brown skin. Past the thoughts that told me I was too pale or imperfect to show my face on this beach, or what did I ever do to deserve to live in such a beautiful place.

When I dove into the endless, ever-deepening blue, it felt like I was leaving my former self behind, right next to my bikini top. I swam out to a big rock near where my friends were already topless and swimming. I perched myself up on the rock like Ariel from *The Little Mermaid,* my face and chest to the sun.

"You're so free!" my friend Aspen said.

"Freer than free," I said and dove back into the water.

DURING THE SEMESTER, I made close friends with Jimmy, a student from South Carolina whose southern drawl was so thick I could barely understand him in English, let alone French. Jimmy was so cheap that he refused to buy sandals and wore his work boots on the beach every day. He would, however, buy limitless beers and mixed drinks.

"Priorities, Shannon," he would say. "Priorities."

He was a fit guy, about my height with dark brown hair and eyes, and a smile that could blow your brains out. I swear, Jimmy could flash you one smile and all of the sad stories stirring in your mind would seep out your ears like murky water. I'd never met anyone like him.

Since I was never very interested in nice, kindhearted guys, our relationship was platonic. Most days on the beach, we'd lean back against a warm rocky wall and look out at the water, each of us sharing one headphone. This tradition began when Jimmy asked me, "What kind of music do you like?" and I gave him the wrong answer: "Everything but country." For the rest of the semester, he made it his mission to get me to fall in love with country music, which he accomplished.

We loved to listen to Tim McGraw's "Live Like You Were Dying." The song was about an older man who received a medical diagnosis that only gave him a certain amount of days to live, so he went mountain climbing and skydiving and bull riding with what time he had left.

Jimmy and I would sit there for an hour sometimes, talking about how much there was to live for and all the places we wanted to travel and the crazy things we wanted to do. While riding a bull was not on my list, I wanted to volunteer at a sanctuary for chimpanzees rescued from biomedical testing, and go bungee jumping, and learn how to ride horses, and write a book, and live in Rome for a year.

I was hungry for life to feed me with excitement and adventure. I wanted to be stimulated. I wanted to be daring and wild. The more good stories I had to tell, the more ground I covered, the more photos I posted online, the more invincible and at the heart of life I hoped to feel.

I didn't have any problems with the extraordinary. It was the ordinary where I ran into trouble: the moments in between the skydives and mountain climbs. When the bars closed and people were sleeping, or on Sunday mornings when the laundry and dishes were piled high, or during the hour between classes, my skin ached and stiffened. My mind raced. All the things that should have never happened and the things that I feared would still happen crammed into my chest so tightly. And then there I was again, walking to the refrigerator, opening the door like some kind of Pandora's Box.

If you looked at my Facebook account, I might have looked like a girl living it up. In every picture I was smiling, surrounded by friends, dancing on the couch of some nightclub or posing in front of a famous landmark. But the truth was that inside, I was always on the run from myself. I needed a loud life to distract me from the harsh voices in my head, from the reality of my internal world.

And so during my time in Europe, I sought after thrill and adventure like never before. I traveled every chance I got—to Italy, Switzerland, the Netherlands, Spain, England, and other parts of France—and with girlfriends who were drop-dead beautiful.

These girls were more than beauty on the surface. They were smart and kind, with layers of depth inside. They had dreams of starting their own businesses, of making a difference in the world, of living in faraway places, of falling in love, and we talked about it all. During the day, I felt an extreme closeness to them, but at night, when it was time to dress up and go out to the clubs, I began to feel different.

If I ate nothing but lettuce and ran for miles and spent an hour on my hair and wore tight outfits that simultaneously showed off my chest and belly-button piercing, I could look in the mirror and convince myself I belonged with this crowd of women. But it was a shaky, vulnerable feeling of belonging, one that could easily be set off-kilter by one *frite* too many or an extra dose of Nutella. Especially on the days I binged and puked, I'd swing to the other end of the spectrum and self-loathing would overtake me. I'd become bad. Fat. The black sheep.

And on my many black sheep nights, I drank to forget the wannabe pretty girl looking back at me in smoky club mirrors. I often woke up the next morning beside a man whose name I didn't know and whose language I didn't speak, remembering little more than a pulsing dance floor and empty martini glasses.

AT THIS TIME, I was the only twenty-year-old virgin I knew. Years earlier, I had promised myself that my first time would be with someone I loved. Unlike most of the promises I made, this one I actually kept. Love was a world I had to admit I was interested in but scared shitless to explore, and yet still, I held on to hope. No matter how drunk I was or how sexy the guy happened to be, a huge danger sign flashed in my mind when it came time to pull out the rubber, and I'd say no.

But one night during spring break, I forgot why saying no mattered to me anymore. My friends and I were at a club in Madrid filled with basically naked girls dancing in cages, when a man named Sebastian bought me a drink. And then a bunch more.

He spoke little English and wore black pants and a fitted shirt that showed off his beefy pectoral and arm muscles. He was maybe ten years older than me, and when he slipped his hands under my skirt and grabbed my ass on the electric blue sex of a dance floor, he didn't know who he was dealing with. Violently insecure girls are sometimes the ones with the tightest outfits, the most makeup, and the dirtiest mouths. We dress to the nines and dance like strippers and talk like we're in bed long before we get there, because the power of feeling desired diffuses our nonstop self-loathing.

"Beautiful," Sebastian would say while he felt my breasts inside my sequined shirt. "Sexy," he'd say with hands around my black miniskirt. And out of all the things I endlessly craved, these words were what I craved the most.

So I left the club with Sebastian at 3 A.M., drunk enough to have only the vaguest recollection about what country I was in. For a brief moment, it occurred to me that I should probably find one of my girlfriends and let them know I was leaving. But it was already too late. Sebastian was pulling me into the back of a cab and removing my panties the instant the door shut behind me. And then we were off on a forty-five-minute drive, most of which I spent straddling Sebastian and begging him to fuck me. Even with the driver present. Even though I'd never had sex before. Even though I'd never behaved this aggressively with a man. Even though I barely knew the guy.

We did just about everything but sex in that cab, Sebastian cursing himself the whole while for having forgotten a condom. He said we couldn't do it without a condom. I said that we could. He said we'd to have wait and I told him I'd been waiting my whole life.

Eventually, we arrived at some palace-like resort and took an elevator up to a rooftop suite. In a grand romantic gesture, Sebastian picked me up and threw me over his back, spanking my ass as he carried me across the living room and bedroom and to the bathroom, which could have easily been mistaken for a luxury spa. I took his shirt off while he set me down on the counter, my back against the mirror.

Sebastian was a strong man with greasy black hair, and he had been rough with me in the car, pulling my hair and biting my lip and squeezing my breasts so hard it hurt. In the bathroom, he continued kissing me like he wanted to suck the life out of me, and then he stripped the rest of my clothes off. He picked me up again and set me down in a shallow tub beneath a marble lion head built into the wall. A marble lion head that I had somehow not noticed until I was sitting directly underneath it. A thick stream of water flowed out of the lion's mouth. I stared at its strange eyes, its mane, its teeth and tongue. "I wash you," Sebastian said with a deep, husky voice. I nodded nervously under marble jaws while he grabbed the loofah.

The lion sobered me up a little. I believe that lion could have sobered nearly anyone up. He reminded me of Scar from *The Lion King,* and his eyes were freakish-looking. While Sebastian scrubbed the inside of my thighs, I counted the lion's teeth. Somewhere around seven, it occurred to me that this was weird. By thirteen, I knew I didn't want to have sex anymore.

Over the next few minutes, Sebastian continued to wash me, and I was thankful for his strange form of foreplay. It gave me time to think, and then to inwardly panic. I mean, I had no idea where I was in Spain. I didn't know Spanish or how Sebastian would react if I said no. He was twice the size of me, hovering over me shirtless with veins popping out of his muscles and with an intensity in his eyes that scared me even more than the lions'.

So I began trying to backpedal. I whispered into Sebastian's ear that I didn't feel well. I said I was tired. Sebastian was too busy washing my crotch and licking the inside of my ears to hear me. All I could think about was how far away I had traveled from my friends, how aggressive I'd been about sex in the car, and now I had to offer up something. I couldn't just leave. Either my ass or my mouth was going to pay, and so I finally climbed out from under the lion and onto my knees and gave Sebastian head with the desperation of a drowning woman. Every time he told me to stop and turn around to have sex, I sucked harder. And when he came, I silently thanked God.

I got into bed and pretended to be asleep until I actually fell asleep. Throughout the night, Sebastian kept trying to have sex with me, and I kept pretending I was sick. I said my head hurt so bad I felt like I was going to die. And I sort of did.

Sebastian sighed and grunted out of frustration and rolled his eyes when I refused sex. He sulked and muttered words I couldn't understand. I could tell he was angry. I could tell he brought a lot of girls home to his luxurious room, and he was used to getting what he wanted.

The next morning, I woke up to the sound of two voices in the living room. One was Sebastian saying the word *bitch*.

I got up, put my clothes back on, and grabbed my clutch and my shoes. I opened the door of the bedroom and found Sebastian standing with a man shorter and skinnier than him, both of them in their underwear. They looked either very angry or very horny, maybe both.

I muttered that I was sorry and made some excuse about how I had to get going, brushing past them without making eye contact. I didn't know exactly what they wanted, but I had an idea.

When I shut the door behind me, I heard the word *bitch* again.

I STOOD OUTSIDE the resort, barely able to stand the smell of myself, all those mixed drinks and Sebastian's greasy hands reeking from my tight black outfit. My head pounded in the bright morning light. I opened my Coach clutch and realized my cell phone was dead. And then I realized that I didn't know the name of the place where my friends and I were staying or what part of town it was in. The only phone number I knew by heart was my mother's.

I stared out at the circular drive and white cabs glaring in the sun, wondering where the hell I would go. And in that moment I missed my mother so much. I didn't feel wild and adventurous anymore. I felt like a little girl in a slutty outfit who would never be able to figure out how to make the voices in her head stop. I felt tired of my aloneness, tired of running, tired of repeating the same mistakes over and over again.

I looked inside the inner pocket of my clutch to see how much money I had left, and wrapped inside of a pink ten-euro bill was a business card with the hostel name and address. I remembered Cristy giving it to me the night before, slipping it into my purse and saying, "In case you get lost . . ."

Cristy was the friend who always had my back, not because she didn't do particularly wild things every now and then but because she cared, because she knew that despite the reckless things I did, I was a good person at heart, and she believed that someday, I'd calm down and be okay.

I wasn't so sure.

10

IN MAY, THE most famous film festival in the world took place in Cannes, as it had for fifty-plus years. The population tripled and prices doubled. Celebrities, paparazzi, and international journalists filled the streets. This was the first time I ever saw a little dog carried in a designer purse, and I called Julie right away to tell her how cute it was.

Back at home, Julie said Mom was talking about filing for divorce from Dad, and high school still sucked, and she was thinking what she needed in life was a kitten. Preferably one with a passport who could fly with her to France.

"Sugar's coming, too," Julie said with a laugh. "And we're all gonna live with you."

"That sounds like a great idea," I said, smiling at the thought of Julie, Sugar, and a kitten making their way through customs.

Then Julie's tone changed and she said, "I miss you. When Dad's drunk and Mom's sad and the girls are bitches at school, I really miss you."

"I miss you, too, Jules," I said, swallowing down a pang of guilt.

.   .   .

DURING THE FESTIVAL, everything in Cannes was about glamour and fashion and sex and dazzling body perfection. Jimmy, who was not allowed into most clubs or parties with his jeans and work boots, hated the festival. He told me not to buy into this "fake shit" for a second, but oh, buy in did I ever.

I wore high heels that made me tower over most men, and a tight black dress with a plunging neckline down to my belly button. Most days I spent prowling and flaunting and flirting for film premiere passes and exclusive invites into parties with friends. We walked around the festival area or Le Suquet, a cobblestone hill with lavish restaurants piled on top of each other, waiting for someone to notice us. Usually, we didn't have to wait long.

During this time, my French teacher announced that amfAR (the Foundation for AIDS Research) was looking for volunteers to help out with their "Cinema Against AIDs" celebrity fund-raising event, and I signed up. My mother shipped an old prom dress and silver stilettos to me, and on the big night, I was assigned to be the assistant to the event director, Ryan. He was a fashionable New Yorker with a charismatic personality, and I took a liking to him right away. Our first task was to manage the red carpet, which essentially meant that Ryan monitored the traffic and kept things moving, while I held his folder and tried not to make an ass out of myself.

We stood at the very front of the carpet and were among the first to see the stars getting out of their limos. At least forty reporters were lined up in a single-file row behind us, holding puffy microphones with their stations' logos, eager to interview. On the opposite side of the carpet, fifty or sixty paparazzi positioned themselves on a stage with bleachers, most of whom were men dressed in black. I could see their arms flailing and people pushing as they tried to get in front. Flashes went off like a miniature fireworks show, minus the booming.

Maybe because everyone around me was reaching with hands and microphones and shouting at the stars, I imagined the red carpet morphing into a river, and I was among those on the banks throwing out hooks, hoping to catch a glimpse of the famous, or even better, a few words.

Celebrities strutted from one microphone to the next, smiling and talking about their latest movies. They made peace signs at the cameras, waved and blew kisses. Sharon Stone, Penelope Cruz, Salma Hayek, Jessica Alba, Brittany Murphy, and the Olsen twins walked by, so beautiful it was almost laughable. Their complexions were perfect. I was close enough to admire their eyelash extensions and shade of lipstick, to smell their perfume and hear the comments they whispered.

Some women twisted their hair around their fingers. Some fixed it nervously. But most beamed with tremendous amounts of confidence and diamonds and gorgeousness. In my Jessica McClintock dress and rhinestone earrings, I felt cheap and dull and ugly. I kept looking at everybody, trying to remind myself that this was all a story. Fiction. Nothing was this perfect. Nothing was this shiny. The famous had secrets, too.

Champagne trays. Fashion. Icons filtering into a tent to raise millions for AIDS research. Smells of French cuisine and competing colognes clashing against each other. Glossy lips moving everywhere. Legs. Women throwing their heads back laughing. Fine skin. Sex. Magic.

High cheekbones. Piercing eyes. Eyes that called to you. Eyes that said, *Ask me anything.* Eyes that said, *You can't come in.*

The men were far less interesting than the women. Only one man I found myself staring at for a long time, and that was because I was trying to decide if he was Hugh Hefner or not. He looked nearly eighty, with three stunning blondes at his side. The girls wore long, glistening gowns with necklines so low they taped the material to their skin so their breasts wouldn't pop out. I could see the tape.

As they made their trek down the carpet, two of the girls were beaming, but the third, the one whose boob tape was the most visible, frowned. Her face, tight with sadness or disappointment, was so striking against all the smiles and veneers passing me by.

It looked to me as if she'd been crying. What was her story? Maybe she just did a line of coke in the bathroom. Maybe she was just tired of being so damn beautiful (was that even possible?). Maybe her father just died, and she was here instead of his funeral. I had no idea, I just knew that something was wrong.

Part of me wanted to tap her on the shoulder and ask if she was okay. Part of me thought she might look at me and say, "You common person, leave me the fuck alone." Part of me was hugely drawn to her, the only person in this sea of glitz and glam who wasn't performing.

AFTER THE STARS had all arrived and walked through the silent auction, I helped to seat them at their tables inside a posh tent where dinner was to be held. Ryan had asked me earlier in the night if there was anyone in particular I was hoping to see, and I had told him Toni Morrison, which was probably odd, because here I was, surrounded by the fanciest celebrities in the world, and I wanted to see a writer of fiction. But of course she wasn't just any writer. She was one of my heroes, and deep down, I was still the high school student who read *The Bluest Eye* over and over again.

Just before dinner began, Ryan called my name over the

walkie-talkie and asked me to come to the entrance of the tent. Then, when I got there, he asked me if I would like to show Ms. Toni Morrison to her table.

She stood less than a foot away from me, with long gray hair in dreadlocks. She breathed and cracked a broad smile so close to me that I could barely think or move. The lights and dinner china all began to sparkle. I can't remember what she was wearing, only that she seemed to sparkle, too. She had an inner calm about her that stood out to me among so many heels and dinner plates rushing all around us. Like the Hugh Hefner model, I could tell that she wasn't pretending. She was genuine. Except in her authenticity, Toni Morrison exuded joy, and a warmheartedness that reminded me of my mother.

When I finally got ahold of myself and motioned for her to follow me to her table, my awareness shifted back to myself, and insecurity flooded my being. I felt not only unprepared for the moment, but unworthy of it in some way.

I took slow steps across the tent, thinking the entire time of what I could possibly say to thank her for her books. I wanted to tell her that I kept quotes from them in my desk and taped to my closet doors at home, and that someday, I wanted to be a writer like her. I wanted to tell her that I loved her, not only for the words she wrote on the page, but for her courage to put them there.

And then we were at her table. I think I pointed to her chair, and Toni Morrison sat down, smiling.

"Thank you," she said.

My mind went: *No. Thank YOU.*

But my mouth wouldn't open to say it. I just nodded and smiled. Then I turned away from my favorite author and left, without telling her what her stories meant to me.

•   •   •

WHEN THE CELEBRITIES were seated, Liza Minnelli performed a song and half the group of student volunteers were allowed to take a quick break. We sat on a stone staircase and were provided with turkey and cheese sandwiches on foot-long baguettes.

While I ate and my dress grew tighter around my stomach, I thought about *The Bluest Eye*'s main character, Pecola, a poor, black girl who believed that the very features I had—blue eyes and white skin—would free her from her suffering. I thought about how I obsessed about losing weight almost as much as Pecola did blue eyes, and what kind of a person that made me.

I'd never been molested or treated badly because of my race. I'd grown up in an alcoholic home, but I'd never been beaten. In fact, I'd been sent to college and to Europe and given opportunities I felt I didn't deserve. In comparison to Pecola, and so many real-life girls, I had it good. More than good. And look at what I did with my life. Look at how unhappy I made myself. Look how I couldn't stop hurting myself though I claimed I wanted to.

When I finished the sandwich, I got up to find a bathroom to get rid of the food (and the self-hatred) inside me that I couldn't stand. But then when I reached the bottom of the staircase, a skinny butterscotch stray cat snuck out from behind the dumpster a few yards to the left of the tent.

An animal was probably the only thing that could postpone my mission to puke. In the same way that my sister couldn't resist diving into the ocean, I couldn't catch a glimpse of an animal, especially one that might be in need, and not investigate further.

I searched for the cat all around the dumpster, which reeked of acidy wine and bad cheese. After a few minutes, I gave up and started heading for the bathroom. But the detour had given me enough time to remember a Toni Morrison quote I wrote with a blue crayon and taped to the front drawer of my desk: "If you surrendered to the air, you could ride it."

Those words pushed against my rib cage and something inside me said, *You don't have to throw up.*

I turned around to find Ryan, still full but suddenly determined to stay that way.

Maybe it doesn't sound like a big deal. But I didn't throw up the sandwich.

This was the first time in my life I didn't do the thing I always did, not because my sister popped out of a bathroom cupboard or because there were too many people around but because an inner guidance compelled me not to.

If I were to look back on my life and draw a line into the sand marking the beginning of my healing, it would be right here. I see myself straddling that line in my royal blue gown, my left foot on the familiar side of self-loathing, but my right foot stepping into new territory, a world where real beauty doesn't strut down a red carpet.

Real beauty rides the air.

11

THE SUMMER AFTER I graduated from college, I woke up before sunrise to kick off a two-week road trip across the country with three friends. Our final destination was a one-story gray house with a red door in San Diego, California, where I hoped to adopt a new, healthier lifestyle as a tan, tofu-eating beach bum. My other plans included finding a surfer-dude boyfriend, becoming the West Coast version of Carrie Bradshaw, and leaving bulimia behind as intentionally as my winter jacket.

Before I left, I crept into my sister's room. At the head of Julie's bed, she'd made a huge collage of photos of us over the years, and beside that, she hung a van Gogh starry night poster I got her from Amsterdam. Julie smelled like hairspray almost constantly now, even in bed, since she was training to become a hairdresser.

Sunny, a ginger kitten Julie recently adopted, was sound asleep on the pillow beside her. He was either purring or snoring, and with good reason, since he'd spent most of the night meowing at the moon and swatting my nose as if it were some tantalizing mouse toy. Sugar tolerated his kitten antics with a saintly amount of patience—sometimes they even slept in her dog bed together. Mom and I, on the other hand, thought

Sunny was a little basket case. He drove us crazy, but he made Julie happy, and that was what mattered.

I leaned over my sister and kissed her forehead, her nose, her cheeks, and her eyelids. I promised to come home soon.

Half-asleep and with her eyes still closed, she whispered that she loved me, too. Then she reached out her arm and drew Sunny in closer.

"Love you more, Jules," I whispered before tiptoeing out the door.

DOWNSTAIRS IN THE kitchen, Mom reminded me for the five hundredth time not to pick up hitchhikers and to always have twenty dollars in cash on me and to call her if I needed anything at all and that I could always come home if I wanted to. We held each other in the kitchen near the humming refrigerator I'd emptied out so many times, and I thanked her for being the best mother that ever was. I told her to tell Dad, who was in a rehab center where Bill Wilson wrote the twelve steps, that I loved him, too.

In the living room, Sugar lay on a pile of pillows on the couch. She was twelve years old now, almost thirteen. I picked her up and cradled her in my arms near the window in the dim morning light. Outside, the sun had risen but the moon still remained in the sky. I felt Sugar's soft white curls against my neck and her slimy pink tongue on my chin and lips. When I said her name, her fluffy white tail swished back and forth in the air.

I told Sugar how much I'd miss her, and I apologized for not having come home from college as much as I should have to walk her in the woods, and I promised her that I'd bring her a cake home from the doggie bakeries I'd heard about in California.

"Goodbye, sweet girl. I love you," I said, brushing her white hair out of her eyes and kissing her small head one last time. Then I set her down on the couch near the front window, unable to look back at her while I opened and shut the front door of the house behind me.

I climbed into my Ford Taurus that was weighed down with heavy bags of books, photos, clothes, and shoes, and then I turned the car and my headlights on. When I pulled out of the driveway, Sugar pushed the window curtains aside with her little black nose, and I saw her sweet eyes gazing out at me through the glass, loving me no matter how far I ran.

12

_____

Two weeks later, after dancing at gay bars in Chicago and eating fried chicken in Kansas and visiting the Grand Canyon in Arizona and nearly hitting a moose in Colorado, my friends and I arrived in Pacific Beach, an infamous party neighborhood in San Diego. The moment we got there, I knew I'd come to the right place. I mean, how, with a vegetarian option at nearly every restaurant, and gyms and yoga centers every few blocks, could I be unhealthy? And how, with all this sunshine to soak up, could I ever be unhappy? And how, among armies of girls riding beach cruisers in bikinis, could I ever feel lonely?

Our house was just a few blocks from the ocean and another few blocks from Garnet Street, where dive bars, tattoo parlors, Forever 21–like stores, coffee shops and nail salons lined up side by side. Hundreds of kids in their teens and twenties flocked there, and every day during happy hour, it was like a high school was dumped upside down right on the road. There were stereotypical platinum-blond girls saying "fer sure" every other sentence and surfers in wet suits balancing surfboards on their heads and grungy kids and angry kids and hippie kids and poet kids and athlete kids and rich kids and homeless kids. Most of us came from somewhere else, walking around in this hectic, giddy place barefoot and sunburnt and naïvely optimistic about the ways California would change our lives.

I saw the California I wanted to see. I didn't see the homeless woman pushing her shopping cart in the alley near my house. I didn't see the dirt and the grit and the pollution. I didn't see that the sun could kiss my skin all it wanted, but I'd still stay hungry inside.

I FOUND A job working as the assistant to the general manager at a hotel, and within the first few months, I started dating Danny, the director of security. He was half-Filipino and in his early thirties, with dark hair and eyes. Unlike the guys I dated in the past (if you can even call it that), there was something more than Danny's looks that attracted me to him—some mix of kindness, maturity, and inner strength. A soulfulness and mystery that drew me into him like a Rumi poem.

As we got to know each other, a passion for animals and R&B music was about all that we had in common. The rest was irony. Danny was impeccably clean, organized, and rational, while I was messy, compulsive, and overly emotional. His father was a winemaker; booze was my father's poison. Danny was a relaxed, positive person while I was insecure and perpetually waiting for shit to hit the fan. But still, I never felt like I belonged with anyone more in my life.

During our first six months together, I kept a journal filled with all the things I loved about him. Here were a few:

1. He treats rain like a special occasion (which I guess it sort of is in San Diego). We light candles and lay down in each other's arms and watch the rain drizzle down the glass.

2. We went camping, and Danny had an allergic reaction to the pollen. Eyes red and glassy, tissues up both nostrils, and still he jammed out to a new John Legend album while making us dinner. I found him sexy as hell.

3. His tan skin turns almost black after a day in the sun.

4. In the ocean, I wrap my arms around his neck and my legs around his waist like a baby monkey, and he wades in the water, carrying me.

5. He often sings Maxwell while in the shower or driving, which could be terrible, but he actually has a good voice.

6. He is so clean and organized that it was a true wonder, a miracle even, that he wants to be with a slob like me.

7. He tells the lamest jokes without an ounce of embarrassment. (Do we have wifi here? I asked the other day. No. But we have because-fi.)

8. Last night, in the middle of a nightmare, I fell off the bed and onto the hardwood floor. When I opened my eyes, Danny was lying right on top of me, his hands cupping my head.

Sometimes Danny and I would lie in bed together for hours, the blades of an old ceiling fan spinning above us. The bed was a queen made of mahogany wood, with eggshell sheets and a white comforter. Danny would put an R&B playlist on Pandora, and I'd put my head on his chest and listen to his heartbeat along with the music. He'd run his hands through my hair. I'd run my fingers around his lips. I'd tell him that he had the longest eyelashes. He'd say that there were gold freckles in my eyes.

We could lie naked in the silence, and I felt comfortable. Danny lived in City Heights, a place few vacationers would choose to visit. Outside the window, there were no palm trees or jacarandas, just barbed-wire fences, dark alleys, burning sun on concrete. Instead of the sound of the ocean, we heard sirens and choppers. And once in the middle of the night, a guy tried to break into our place. Danny chased him away with a gun.

Still, I felt safer in Danny's arms and in that shabby apartment than anywhere else in the world. Especially alone with myself.

WHEN YOU FALL in love with someone, you fall in love with the best parts of them first. I fell in love with Danny's looks and sex and quirkiness and positivity and downright heroic attempts to make me laugh. In the beginning, it was all about his deep brown eyes and the giddy feeling I got looking into them.

As far as I was concerned, he was perfect, and I wanted him to think the same of me. The last thing I wanted him to know was that despite moving across the country, I still had a little problem with inhaling three pizzas at a time and throwing up.

So I tried to present to Danny only the sides of myself I believed he could love: my creativity and sense of adventure. I exaggerated stories to make him laugh harder. I behaved in the most thoughtful of ways so that he could never guess how wrapped up in myself I was when he wasn't looking. I kept my bulimic life so guarded that I began to feel like two girls living in the same (never thin enough) body.

The thrill of falling in love and the comfort of being in his arms distracted me from the voices continually sweet-talking my fingers down my throat, and somehow, I managed to never binge or puke or cry in Danny's presence. It was only when I was alone, back in Pacific Beach, that I ate massive amounts of food and bruised my knees on cold, cracked tile floors and hugged toilet bowls in the dark.

So after years of keeping myself sheltered from any intimate relationship, I now was on the other end of the spectrum, afraid to be apart from Danny, wanting him to protect me from myself. After just a month together, I started to spend every weekend at his place. Then I'd come home to my beach house on Monday to the same bills and urge to eat elephant-sized portions and fears of getting hurt and fucking up.

This is how I learned that falling in love would not turn my life into a fairy tale or obliterate all the darkness. Because alongside my love for Danny was my potent self-hatred and all-consuming fear that in the end, deep down, I was unlovable. Wrapped up in my love for him were the sickness and lies and shame I was convinced I could never tell him about.

13

OUR FAVORITE DOG beach was in Ocean Beach, a hippie section of San Diego filled with Bob Marley posters, locally grown organic, usually vegan products, palm readers, peace signs, marijuana, and long-haired surfer dudes who'd worshipped the water all their lives. I doubted there were many Republicans in the area, and you quickly got the sense that the people of this town loved gay people as much as straight people, punk rock fans as much as techno lovers, pit bulls as much as poodles, and beer pong as much as surfing. No matter how melancholy I was, this eccentric place, and its dog beach in particular, the first official leash-free dog beach in America, always lifted my spirits. You walked past a popular do-it-yourself dog wash and a few beach volleyball nets, and then just over a rocky pier: enough dogs and people of every breed and creed to eat your heart out.

One lazy summer morning, four months after Danny and I started dating, we sipped coffee on the sand and watched happy mutts run all around us. Our favorites were the inexhaustible ones, the ones who charged like missiles into the waves to retrieve sticks and worn tennis balls like they were the most precious objects in the world. They came back to shore dripping salt water and beaming with self-satisfaction, eager for another throw. There was just something so uninhibited and beautiful about it, something that made you ask yourself, *Why can't I charge into the great unknown like that?*

But not all the dogs at OB Dog Beach were water dogs. One black and white husky loved to sit at an unoccupied lifeguard booth high above everyone else. One pit bull loved to dig in the sand until only his butt and wagging tail were visible aboveground. There was a golden doodle who, once she was good and dirty, ran up to every person sitting on the beach and bear-hugged them. She bathed their faces in kisses whether they liked it or not. When people saw her coming they'd stand up, but I never did. I loved being ambushed by that adorable, sandy beast.

Danny and I sat down near the black-and-white husky and his lifeguard station. He pointed out in the distance a regular who we loved to watch, a little Jack Russell confused about his status as a dog (he believed he was a fish). He loved swimming so much that when his owner lifted him out of the water (because he never came out willingly), he'd start dog-paddling in her arms, swimming in the air as she carried him to shore, as if in utter refusal to believe he was out of the ocean.

I took a sip of my lukewarm coffee and set it down. Then I hugged my knees and dug my toes in the sand, trying to muster up the courage to tell Danny what I'd decided.

Over the past few months, I shared, in tolerable bits and pieces, the facts of my eating disorder, but Danny was beginning to figure out some things on his own. He said that sometimes at night he heard me talking about my father in my sleep. A week ago, he said that it was like my body was here but my mind wasn't, and that's how I felt after a night I binged and purged. Barely human. A vessel of want and hunger and nothing else.

Some nights in Pacific Beach, I moved like a zombie from one fast-food joint to the next, and puked in a McDonald's bathroom or near the ocean. I woke up not only exhausted and disgusted with myself, but at a loss for why I couldn't just go to bed and stay there like my roommates. They were getting tired of my lies, and I thought it was just a matter of time before Danny would, too.

The fear of him leaving me and the anxiety of living a double life and the crack of humility that had widened ever since I realized that no matter how far I ran, bulimia raced beside me, had finally cornered me into some clarity, and I realized I had two options:

1. I could either continue to grow sicker while hopelessly trying to heal myself, or
2. I could go to rehab and place my healing into the hands of others with more sanity and wisdom than me.

Selecting the second option was the bravest thing I've ever done, but at the time, I felt like a colossal failure, and I worried that Danny would think I was, too. With all my therapy appointments and self-help books and antidepressants and yoga classes, I didn't know why I couldn't just get my shit together and be happy. And I certainly didn't know how to explain it to Danny.

After a few minutes of tossing and turning in my mind, applying sunscreen to my shoulders, braiding my hair—putting off the inevitable—I finally turned to him. My throat tightened. I clenched and unclenched fistfuls of sand in my hands. Then I said, "So, I think I need to go to rehab."

"I think that's a good idea," Danny said, looking right into my eyes. There was a touch of relief in his voice, as though he'd been hoping for this. He draped one arm around my shoulder and drew me closer to him. I stared down at my tan, out-stretched legs.

"I think I need to go somewhere I'll be monitored twenty-four/seven," I continued. "Because I can't trust myself."

Danny nodded and placed his hand on top of mine to stop me from scratching my leg. Then he traced his fingers along my knuckles in a soothing gesture.

"And I know that means you can't trust me," I said. "But honey, I'll tell you anything you want to know right now. I'll tell you—"

"I don't need to know how bad it is," Danny interrupted, his eyes harder now. "But you do. You need to know that things have gotten bad enough if anything is ever going to change. Or you're just going to waste everything."

By everything, I knew he meant not only my health or life but us.

I stared out at the shoreline, which was a long mirror re-flecting the sky and clouds and sun. The shallow water was like chrome-colored paint with hundreds of paws splashing around in it.

And in that moment, I could see so clearly that I didn't want to waste everything.

Even if I had to be hospitalized. Even if I could never be that bone-thin woman in my sick dreams. Even if healing from this disease would be the hardest thing I'd ever do, I wanted to do it. I had to do it. So that I could continue my relationship with this man that I loved. So that I could come to places like this, surrounded by dogs, rejoicing without leashes. So that I could live a life worth living.

Eventually, we got up and took a walk by the water. Nearby,

a little terrier-poodle mix with gray-and-white stringy fur caught our attention.

"Look," Danny said. "He's playing with the waves, like play bowing at them."

The dog would wait in eager anticipation of a breaking wave with his chest down, rear up, tail wagging. The instant a wave began to cave over itself, he'd charge toward it and dive into the crashing water. He would get tossed around a bit but then surface moments later with this wildly happy, proud look on his face. He would come back to the beach covered in sea muck and get into the same play bow position, looking more determined than ever, as if to say, *Come on, ocean. Give me what you've got.*

He seemed so unintimidated by the ocean, so fearless and oblivious to his size, that it made me painfully aware of how different we were.

14
___

A FEW MONTHS LATER in August, a white van drove me up a long and dusty driveway to the Rosewood Centers for Eating Disorders in Wickenburg, Arizona. In the distance, everything was lifeless and dead quiet and some shade of brown, except for the clusters of cotton-candy clouds gliding across a luminous sky. The temperature was in the hundreds and sweat gathered on the back of my neck the instant I stepped outside.

A nurse walked me into an old and mercifully air-conditioned one-story ranch where all my possessions were sorted through. My money, medicine, and books were set aside in a plastic bag to be returned to me when I was released a month later. I knew well enough not to bring anything sharp.

The intake room was white and sterile, except for the small oak table, which looked like it might belong in a quaint log cabin rather than a hospital. I sat at the table and filled out paperwork for the next twenty minutes, signing away my freedom. From that point on nurses would monitor me in the bathroom (standing right outside the door to listen for gagging sounds) and hover over me at every meal. They'd make sure I had one packet of salt, pepper, or Mrs. Dash per serving (eating-disordered people have a tendency to overdo it on these things, to make their tasteless diet of lettuce a bit tastier). If I didn't finish my plate at mealtime, I'd have to drink protein shakes (a pink, milky Pepto-Bismol-like formula). No caffeine was allowed, no exercise, no books unless they were related to recovery, no bikinis, just one-piece bathing suits patients wore in the small community swimming pool. Some mirrors were covered in butcher paper to prevent "body checking," or scrutinizing and obsessing about your reflection.

After I filled out the last of my forms, I was escorted to the dining hall, where about twenty other female patients were gathered for lunch. Half the room was filled with long wooden tables, and the other half was more like a living room with cluttered bookshelves, couches, and beanbags. Affirmations written in crayon by patients on pieces of construction paper were taped to the walls. A big poster near the door read: "The Scale Can Never Tell Me How Loved I Am!"

Several women were in wheelchairs because malnourishment had caused edema, making their calves flare up like balloons. Most patients were in their twenties or thirties, but there were a few teenagers and elderly women. Just five years later, Rosewood would develop an adolescent recovery program—parents calling in hopes to admit children as young as eight years old.

The majority of patients were anorexic rather than bulimic like me, because it was nearly impossible to get insurance coverage with a healthy body mass index (BMI). At 150 pounds, I immediately noticed that I was the second-heaviest girl in the room. I didn't want to end up so thin I needed a wheelchair, but more than any other desire living inside my chest, I wanted to be thirty pounds lighter.

A nurse sat at the head of each of the tables, where every patient had an assigned seat marked by a half sheet of laminated lime-green and hot pink paper. Before we ate what looked like a

Thanksgiving meal—turkey, potatoes, all the trimmings—we flipped our name sheets over to read a prayer on the back:

"What is in front of me meets my needs. I will accept this food as nourishment for my body and mind. May my life be enriched by these gifts I am receiving."

The frail southern belle next to me, who was perhaps seventy, unenthusiastically muttered the words like a child sick of saying the pledge of allegiance. She wore a dress and a necklace made of turquoise rocks. I could imagine her putting it on in the morning and falling over, the weight of the necklace crushing her tiny body. On the other side of me was a tan woman in her thirties who looked like a retired *Playboy* playmate. With the exception of her busty implants, which she showed off in a low-cut T-shirt, the rest of her skeletal body fought with gravity, her orange skin hanging off bone.

Across the table from me was a girl in her twenties, so underdeveloped and thin that she looked like one of those children on a late-night commercial, ones we can feed for only pennies a day. She pinched her lips together as if that would keep her from having to eat the food before her.

So maybe to show her something or maybe to show myself something, I picked up my fork and knife and silently gave thanks, and I started to eat.

After I washed my last bite down with some milk, ten chairs skirted on the floor behind me. There was a loud belching sound, and then somebody screamed, "Oh God, no!"

I turned around and a teenage Indian girl had projectile-vomited her lunch across the table. It reeked and threatened to have a contagious effect as other patients hunched over themselves, covering their mouths and gagging. I stood up and looked away.

The teenager was promptly escorted out of the room by two nurses on either arm. She kicked her skinny legs, wailing, "I didn't do it on purpose! I promise I didn't do it on purpose!"

I felt sorry for her but also jealous. I would have given anything right then to throw up in secret.

I went to the bathroom after the meal, a nurse right outside the door, listening for gagging sounds.

MY FIRST NIGHT, I slept (or attempted to sleep) in a room with six cots next to the nursing unit. I was exhausted but a ghostlike woman in her sixties with long gray hair in the cot beside me kept getting up throughout the night. She got in and out of bed, roaming around the room as if sleepwalking. Her eyes seemed so lost and unsettled, reminding me of an abandoned German shepherd looking for its owner, desperate for a smell that was long gone. Sometimes she just sat on the edge of her cot with her spindly legs dangling in the air, staring at the white wall. Nurses were constantly coming back in to put her back to bed, and I was constantly cursing her in my mind, thinking that she loved the attention.

Even without the shepherd woman, though, I would have had a hard time sleeping. While I had done well eating the meals required, now that the lights were out and I was alone with my body, I retreated into familiar patterns. I pinched the skin around my stomach and thighs, feeling like I'd gained twenty pounds in twelve hours.

I told my body that I hated it. I had conversations with my perceived love handles and fat ass and round face all the time. Alone at night or in front of bathroom mirrors, I spit out words of disgust. (If only I had learned to have some conversations with my heart then . . . *What makes you feel alive?* I'd ask. *What hurts? What feels right?*)

The last thing I remember before falling asleep was thinking about how fat I was, squeezing the flesh on my arms, trying to gauge how much weight I had actually gained that day. I told myself that I would learn what I needed to learn here, but I would never eat the way they were telling me to eat when I got out of this place. Not this much food. Not this often.

AT 7 A.M., my name was called for "Morning Vitals." Light poured in through the windows and I begrudgingly changed out of Danny's T-shirt into a white paper gown. I wanted to sleep more. I wanted coffee. I wanted to kiss Danny. I wanted to kill the shepherd-eyes woman, who was now sleeping peacefully. Apparently, it wasn't her turn yet for vitals.

I followed a nurse across the hall to a freezing cold, windowless room. The nurse wasn't a pretty woman, but her teeth were straight and white enough to make me wonder if they were bleached. She had pale green eyes and bright purple scrubs on, looking far too colorful for this place.

After closing my eyes and stepping on the scale (we weren't allowed to know our own weight), I sat down on a table padded with the butcher paper. An air conditioner hummed somewhere in the background. The nurse took my temperature and looked inside my eyes, ears, and mouth. I was self-conscious of my breath, as I hadn't brushed my teeth yet.

She asked me questions about how I felt physically. I listened and responded politely, even though hate crawled in my blood. All I could think about was how I didn't want to be weighed every day in this stupid paper gown, how I didn't want to be around these women moving peas around their plate like children and tottering on bony legs and weeping in wheelchairs.

"I need to take your blood now," the nurse said, asking for my arm.

My irritation melted into fear. I bit my lip and anxiously told the nurse how much I hated giving blood. "Is it really necessary?" I pressed.

"It will just take a minute. I promise I'm very good at this."

I don't care if you're good at this. I don't want to do it.

She tightened an elastic band around my arm and tried to distract me. "So, where are you from?" she asked.

"California," I said. I stared at the white wall in the opposite direction.

"Oh, I've been there once. I love the ocean, so peaceful."

I took a deep breath and braced myself for the prick of the needle, telling myself not to be a wuss, but still the knee-jerk reaction happened anyway. Just before she inserted the syringe, I pulled my arm away and hissed, "No!"

The nurse gave me a gentle smile, seeming a little entertained by my response. I held my arm near my chest, feeling stupid.

"You weren't kidding, huh?" she said. "It's okay, dear. Let's just talk for a minute. Okay?"

"Okay."

"Do you have any brothers or sisters?" she asked.

"One."

"Brother or sister?"

"Sister. Her name is Julie."

I thought of Julie then as a child. At our doctor's appointments, I always made her go first whenever we needed shots. She'd stick her skinny arm out and say, "See, Shan, it's not scary." Then when the needle was inserted, she'd smile in an effort to show me it wasn't so bad, the right side of her lip curling up more than her left.

For the past twenty-four hours, I hadn't talked much and kept to myself. I walked around quietly nodding my head and doing what I was told. But now I found myself telling the nurse how much I missed my sister. How in my eyes, she'd always been the stronger one of the two of us.

"Maybe, when your time gets hard here, you can think of Julie," the nurse said. "Think of how it will be to spend time with her with this awful disease off your back. Think of how much more present you'll be."

Even though she was trying to help me, what I heard was that I had not been present for Julie, the little girl with watery blue eyes who was now battling her own demons as an adult. Her story is not mine to tell, but suffice it to say that she'd recently needed me in a big way, and I hadn't been there. She needed someone now to make her less afraid, to hold out their arm and take a shot for her first. But I was busy in California puking my brains out.

To be there for Julie without the background noise of food obsession—I'd never let myself imagine it before. Perhaps because I couldn't imagine it. And at that thought, a bomb of tears went off in the center of my chest. There was no way to redirect the emotion, nothing I could stuff into my mouth or force out of my body to make me forget how ashamed I was.

All I could do was sit in the arms of a nurse I never learned the name of, sobbing into her warm shoulders for five minutes, maybe ten. I cried so hard that tears fell down my face and made my paper gown translucent in some places, the material ripping.

She held me tight as the waves of grief passed through me. I felt like if I needed to sit there and cry for another hour in her arms, she would have let me.

But I didn't cry for another hour. I finally lifted my head and wiped my eyes and extended my arm. For the first time in my life, I stared directly at the syringe.

I watched the dark blood seep out of me.

OUT OF ALL the rehabs I looked at, I chose Rosewood based on the picture of a dark brown horse with a white star in between his eyes, which I found on the Equine Therapy page of Rosewood's website. I had scanned dozens of rehabs across the country with all their shiny promises, but it was the picture of this horse I kept coming back to, him and his black joy-lit eyes.

Equine therapy was about the only thing I'd been looking forward to at Rosewood, and during my first session, I stood with a handful of patients and our therapist, Heather, inside of an old wooden fence. Heather was a tall, beautiful, tough woman whose presence immediately commanded respect. While touching her long blond braid, which looped around over her shoulder, she introduced us to a pony named Rosie, and two large horses: Chico and Poncho.

For the first few minutes, we just observed the horses. I loved the clop of their hooves on the ground and the dust clouds that rose up when they trotted. I loved their sinewy bodies and the gentleness of their mouths on the palm of my hand. What I loved most about the horses was what I loved most about all animals—the immediacy of their lives. Life was one continuous experience of the now, and they felt everything in the moment. The tangerine sun on their backs. The delicate touch of a fly's legs on their eyelid. The hay they chomped on with block teeth between thick charcoal lips. The appearance of a person, the crunch of a carrot, the sensation of fresh water moving down their throats and into their bellies.

Heather explained to us that the larger horses had been rescued from slaughter. They were rejects from the racing industry because of some flaw in their bodies, which of course was a metaphor she went wild with, talking about how we were more than our bodies, how we had to stop damaging ourselves because of perceived flaws or imperfections.

I was sort of listening, but all my attention was wrapped up in Chico, whose warm, broad chest I pressed my hand against. I felt his lungs breathing in and out, in and out.

I could see my own reflection in his black pupils. My cheeks weren't puffy after just a few nights without vomiting. My lips weren't chapped. My hair was pulled back and my face was almost childlike without makeup.

I liked this girl I was seeing.

That was my last thought before I felt a sudden rush of heat to the head and everything became liquid: the sky, the dirt, the horses, the patients. Dehydrated and hot in the morning sun, I fainted, my head landing in the dirt near Chico's right front hoof.

When I came to, I remember thinking how clean and velvety it looked for being in the dirt all day long. Stars swirled around it. The air was made up of a hundred million bright specs. Translucent confetti. How massive Chico was to me in that moment. How godlike. How beautiful. I heard myself saying the words, *Yes, I'd eaten breakfast. No, I hadn't brought water.* I vaguely heard people around me, but I couldn't take my eyes off the muscular shadow of his body set against an oceanic sky. I'd never felt so small in my life.

•   •   •

YEARS LATER, I would experience that sensation of smallness again, and with another equine therapy horse. I worked for a local humane society then, and Dixie worked at the Therapeutic Equestrian Activity Center for the Handicapped, or "TEACH." She was as tall as Chico had been and chestnut brown, with a wide strip of white stretching from the center of her eyes to her nostrils. She had been rescued by our Humane Investigations team a few months earlier, and I'd heard the situation was dire: neglected, abused, terrified, severely malnourished, hauntingly familiar to some of the patients I met at Rosewood, flesh hanging off bone.

But the horse I found myself now filming looked anything but weak. She stood strong and beautiful, a white pearl sun in the sky behind her. A little girl named Faith was lifted up off the dirt and placed onto a pink blanket on Dixie's saddle. Faith looked about five years old, with long, light brown hair pulled back in a ponytail, and a pale blue T-shirt on. A patch of sunlight reflected off her black helmet wherever Dixie took her.

Faith and Dixie completed a lap around the ring, and everybody applauded them. Faith beamed a big smile and let out a squeal of joy that reminded me more of a puppy than a child, but perhaps that was because I was around a lot more puppies than children.

I squatted down low in the dirt to take a picture of Faith raising her arms to the sky while riding Dixie, and I felt that same sensation of smallness I experienced at Rosewood.

It had less to do with the physical size of my body, and more to do with realizing the smallness of my perception, how I often viewed life from the same pent-up angle, the same narrow filter.

When did I ever notice clouds moving in the sky, light

flickering through the trees, a warmth tingling inside my own body? When did I ever see that even a lightbulb or a rain puddle could pulse with beauty? When did I ever look at anything, like a girl named Faith riding a rehabilitated horse, and think, *What wisdom are you here to teach me?*

15

AFTER JUST TWO days of treatment, I was pulled out of a nutritionist session where we were learning portion sizes with pretend food. I set down the rubber hamburger patty and a plastic banana I was holding on the table, and followed a therapist into a sterile back office, where she told me that my insurance had dropped coverage.

Apparently, I wasn't sick enough to be there. My BMI, which had not changed in forty-eight hours, now made me ineligible.

I remember arguing that a stable weight did not equal a stable mind and begging the therapist to let me stay, as if she could do something to change my fate. I remember calling my mother and then my sister and telling them both that I was scared. I even called my father, who had been in rehab for twenty-one days in Connecticut, and who said, "Honey, we're going to figure this out. You're going to get through this. I love you."

But most of all, I remember feeling exactly like I did when I didn't make the dance team in college, or when I got a B-plus average on my report cards in high school. I was a good dancer but not great. I was a good student but not great. Now I was a good bulimic but not great. Rosewood was a top-notch facility for bulimics and anorexics and I didn't make the cut.

That night, I was transferred to a "step down" facility fifteen minutes down the road, sort of like a sober house for girls with eating disorders. Rosewood Capri had been converted from an old, one-story, L-shaped motel. Even in the dark, I could tell the place was run-down. Patient rooms hugged a big black parking lot near a tiny pool behind a silver fence where the water was always slightly green. Inside a small building where most of my time would be spent, there were two kitchens where patients prepared meals, a dining room, and group and individual therapy rooms.

Over the next three weeks, I followed directions and did what I was supposed to, treating the whole experience as I did school, striving for straight A's. I went to individual and group therapy and nutritionist appointments. I went to a Christian church and cried my eyes out at the sound of gospel music. I made chocolate-covered strawberries. I made chicken parmesan. I made meatballs. I wrote a letter to my disease, telling it to fuck off. I wrote another letter to my disease, telling it how I couldn't live without it.

I went on a field trip to McDonald's, where I huddled in a booth with three patients, each of us forced to eat hamburgers and tell a therapist how it made us feel. (I wanted to ask the therapist how she felt after eating a greasy burger and fries . . . did she feel good? Did she feel like she was ready to take on the world?)

I visualized being naked and alone with my body during guided meditations. I taped cards to the walls by my bed sent from college friends, my mom and sister, my aunt Libby. I drank a lot of decaf coffee (caffeine was still not allowed). I prayed to a god I didn't believe in. I prayed that the golden retriever whom

Heather once brought to group therapy and who sat beside me on the floor and let me lean into him and stroke his soft, yellow fur, would come back for another session. But he never did.

I meditated morning and night, striving to count my breath in and out up to ten, over and over again. I did tai chi. I did Reiki. I used measuring cups and scales to determine the food I was supposed to eat, how much cereal to go in my bowl or ounces of turkey in my sandwich. Not even once did I think about skimping out on portion sizes or puking up the food I ate.

I think this was because even though nobody was designated to watch over my eating habits, I still felt like people were. Therapists and doctors and nurses were around constantly, and as different as this place was from the ranch, I was still incarcerated. I couldn't leave when I wanted to. I had to follow the specific schedule of therapeutic activities each day, or I'd get kicked out. Getting kicked out meant starting back at square one, and that wasn't an option for me. I decided that if I couldn't keep myself from vomiting here, then I couldn't do it anywhere. I counted the days I went without purging like sober people count the days of their sobriety, marking each day on a calendar with a glittery heart sticker that made my real heart do a little backflip. The more days I counted, the more cohesive my thoughts became and the stronger my body felt.

AT CAPRI, I continually compared myself to the patients who were puking or visibly struggling to follow the rules, and I pitied them.

One patient who was supposed to be admitted to Capri died the day before she arrived. I have a vague memory of the doctors saying that she had a heart attack in her parents' home, but that could be wrong. There are lots of ways a bulimic can die: ketoacidosis (when high acid levels build up in your blood, leading to a sudden coma or death), pancreatitis, cardiac arrest, gastric rupture, hypoglycemia, hyperglycemia, seizures. Eating disorders have the highest mortality rate of any mental illness.

"This is a fatal disease," one of the doctors said as she told us the news. "It could easily take any of you."

I remember sitting in the semicircle of women with the ugliest quilt wrapped around myself and thinking, *Not me. It will never take me.*

I didn't recognize then that I was developing the same kind of confident attitude that Dad had around his drinking. Every time he got out of the hospital or rehab, he was sure he was done for good, and yet he sometimes found himself stopping at a bar before he even made it home. My overconfidence speaks to the fact that I still did not understand the power and tenaciousness of the illness I was up against. After just weeks of some abstinence from eating-disordered behaviors, I lost touch with the kind of primal desperation that caused me to consider that maybe I did not have all the answers.

I thought I was going to return to San Diego and go on just fine, armed with my meal plans and meditation and tai chi practice and all that I'd learned. I didn't know that while I was unlikely to end up in a wheelchair with edema and a tube down my throat anytime soon, I was still on a hopeless path, still trapped in a desperate place of hunger for praise and validation, which would keep me focused on the external world rather than the internal one, which would keep me dressing well but spiritually and emotionally bankrupt, which would keep me trapped in a body I hated, ever needing the approval of others, ever wishing to be somebody else.

The remedy for that—I still hadn't found.

PART
TWO

"You will learn a lot about yourself if you stretch in the direction of goodness, of bigness, of kindness, of forgiveness, of emotional bravery. Be a warrior for love."

—CHERYL STRAYED

16

WHEN I RETURNED from Rosewood, I stood on the curb of the airport and inhaled a deep breath of sweet ocean air. Sunlight warmed my shoulders and a gentle breeze blew through my hair. Of all birds, a seagull perched himself on the bench beside me. Among the buzz of people coming and going, rushing and waiting—the impatient horns and bright lights—I felt a wonderfully euphoric sense of unimportance. I'd sent in my resignation letter to the hotel from Rosewood, so there was no job to go back to. No weighty responsibility looming over me.

Danny's car pulled to the curb and in seconds we were holding each other, saying, *I love you. I've missed you.*

He wore a blue button-down shirt, different from his usual, more casual Saturday T-shirts. I dressed up for the occasion, too, straightening my hair and using the makeup I didn't touch during my days at Rosewood. When I poured foundation out of the glass bottle and onto my fingertips, the color was too dark. I'd actually gotten paler in the desert, all that time indoors trying to heal.

Danny drove home with one hand on the wheel and the other on my leg. He said that he missed my face, my laugh, even my nervousness. I said how much I missed his voice and his bad jokes and sleeping in his arms. He played a CD of new music he'd made for me, and the bass bumped beneath our seats as we drove past the ocean, which looked bluer than ever to me after so much time staring out at dust. Danny said that he also went grocery shopping to make sure we had lots of healthy food back at the apartment. His thoughtfulness stung in my chest a little, especially since Danny lived on a mostly fast-food diet.

Back at the apartment, a tall glass vase of Stargazer lilies sat on the nightstand. The milky white petals looked like feathers, speckled with tiny pink dots at the center. A small note beside the vase read, "*So proud of you, Welcome Home.*"

Danny and I lie in bed, the ceiling fan slicing and spreading the aroma around us. White Stargazers are known to symbolize innocence and purity, and in Danny's arms, I remember feeling like the past had been erased and I was clean again.

Light spilled onto us from the musty window, and I looked into Danny's eyes and said, "I never want to go back to how it was."

"You don't have to," he said, kissing my forehead.

TIME SUDDENLY FELT roomy rather than cluttered with things to do. There seemed to be so many more hours in the day, not only because I worked short shifts at a local bookstore rather than long days at the hotel, but because my obsession around food had lessened. The smallest things suddenly felt so beautiful and important, swirling half-and-half and real sugar in my coffee instead of skim milk and Splenda, closing my gym membership, waking up and thinking about what I wanted to do rather than what to eat, making love with the lights on, opening my eyes in the shower, sleeping through the night.

Danny had left the hotel to start his own security business, which was taking off fast. While he sometimes worked ten- or twelve-hour days, I filled my time with a lot of therapy, nutritionist appointments, and hours spent at the San Diego Zoo, just a few miles from our apartment. Twice, sometimes even three times a week, I'd come home with a hundred photos of animals on my phone, never able to emphasize quite enough to Danny just how amazing it was when the baby gorilla pressed his hand to my hand on the glass, or when the elephant gave herself a bath, or when the polar bear tossed a red ball in the air.

He'd just smile and say, "I'm glad you've found a new addiction."

We both agreed this one was much better.

Sometimes I spent hours at the zoo admiring the great apes—the gorillas, orangutans, and the less well known bonobos. Bonobos look a lot like chimpanzees, but their societies are uniquely peaceful because they resolve all problems through sex rather than fighting (the things animals can teach us!). Just like with humans, sex transcends reproduction purposes and serves as pleasure for them. Bonobos are one of the most intelligent, sensitive, and expressive species in the world, and yet still, they are nearing extinction due to poaching and logging in the Democratic Republic of the Congo, the only place left where they exist in the wild.

One day while I watched these beautiful creatures, a man with a potbelly and passion for the rain forest told me a story. A week earlier, he witnessed two bonobo sisters being reunited here at the zoo after being separated for thirty years.

"They were placed on opposite sides of this exhibit," he said, raising his hands to point at either end. "The moment their handlers let them go, they sprinted to and wrapped their arms around each other like they'd been waiting forever to be together again. They've been joined at the hip ever since."

Sure enough, in the corner of the exhibit, two bonobo monkeys sat under the shade of a tree, looking into each other's eyes with intense concentration. They touched each other's mouths and noses and earlobes. They held hands. Their lips moved as though they were having an intimate conversation that only two sisters could have. I imagined them saying, "Let's never go this long without seeing each other again. I'll miss you terribly."

When I walked home from the zoo that day, I called my own sister and told her the story.

She said, "I'd superglue myself to your back before I let myself be separated from you that long. That's bullshit. Sisters have to stay together."

I DON'T THINK my passion for animals ever left me, but that sort of passion lives in the heart, and an eating disorder clutters up the mind, throwing out horrible mental traffic and making the connection between mind and heart a road so filled with potholes and detours that I got confused about who I was. I got confused about what I loved. I got confused about where I belonged.

I remember one time, when I was working at the hotel, I stepped into a glammed-up ballroom and announced that the designer table linens looked "stunning." In reality, I thought they were ludicrously expensive, shit-brown napkins, but I went on and on about how gorgeous they were.

Kissing was stunning. The yellow eyes of a coyote were stunning. Two bonobo sisters reunited was stunning. But for the love of God, table linens were not.

So while after Rosewood I still cared a lot about what people thought, I was tired of pretending to be someone I wasn't. I had more clarity about what I longed for, and it was not the hospitality business. I decided that I'd work at the bookstore making minimum wage until I found a job that actually meant something to me. I even interviewed for a job in the public relations department at the zoo, but I didn't get it.

After I got over that heartbreak, Danny heard of a position for marketing coordinator at a local humane society, and I applied that very night.

17

THE FOLLOWING WEEK, after my sister's graduation from hairdressing school, Mom returned home to the nightmare she'd been dreading. She said that when she opened the front door, Sugar fell hard while trying to drag herself up off the floor to greet her. Mom knelt down beside her in the foyer and gently touched her front leg, which was broken. Sugar's eyes were bleary and her breath was shallow. She could barely lift her head, let alone kiss my mother as she always did. Mom knew the time had come.

Julie rushed home and went with my mother to the vet. After Sugar was given medication for the pain, Julie spent an hour saying goodbye to her in a sterile back room. Earlier that day, she beamed like someone who had just won a million dollars. Now Julie sat down on the floor with Sugar breathing heavy in her lap. Black lines of mascara ran down her cheeks. Her dangly earrings tangled in her red hair. Julie cupped Sugar's small paws, pressed her forehead to Sugar's forehead, and thanked her for being the greatest dog that ever lived.

"You're the most loving dog in the world," Julie said again and again. And it was true. While we might have outlived her, Sugar had outloved us all.

Julie didn't want to be there during Sugar's last moments,

and so in the end, it was my mother and her white shadow, the loving presence that followed Mom from room to room, the comfort that Mom counted on during all these years of instability. Mom cradled her in a blanket, kissing the top of her head. She whispered in a reassuring voice that it was okay for her to go now, that she was a good girl, a very good girl. She looked into Sugar's eyes and they seemed tired and confused, but not afraid. Sugar had spent more time in Mom's arms than any dog bed over the years, and she seemed content to be there now.

After the vet inserted the syringe into a vein in Sugar's leg, Mom felt Sugar's lungs exhale their last breath. She pressed her finger to Sugar's black nose, and while it was still wet, air had stopped flowing through her nostrils. Mom used to say that when Sugar was sniffing a bush, she was reading a story. Now there were no more stories to read. Mom buried her face into Sugar's fur and cried.

Mom had tried to get ahold of me earlier, but I was working a shift at Borders and my phone was off. I spent most of the shift avoiding one of my bosses, who treated alphabetizing books like some kind of military operation, and when I got into my car and saw Mom's missed calls, I called her back immediately. She answered while still holding Sugar's lifeless body in the vet's office, and I knew by the sound of her voice that it had already happened.

It was a rare rainy day in San Diego, and the sky itself looked sickly. I pulled over to the side of the road and wept over my steering wheel while raindrops gathered and made mini-rivers on my windshield.

We stayed on the phone for a few minutes, crying too hard to speak. I thought of the couch near the front window of our house where she always waited for us to come home, her little black nose pushing the curtains aside. I remembered the first time I held her as a three-pound puppy, parading her around the neighborhood in a wagon as kids, rushing her to the vet when she swallowed the bee, and lying in bed with her in the middle of the night as a teenager, my nose pressed to her wet nose. Sugar never called me a drama queen and jumped off the bed. Instead, she nestled her head into the crease of my neck, licking my mouth and my tears.

While I may have taught Sugar "sit" and "down" and "shake," all her life she tried to teach me the trick of lying back and letting go. Of letting happiness reveal itself to me, rather than chatting in my mind all day long about what I needed to be happy. For almost fourteen years, she let the world amaze her, stir her, inspire her to run in crazy circles. She drank up the love my family gave her without ever questioning if she deserved it. She accepted each of us for who we were within ourselves, not for what we looked like. Her only complaint in life was for more kibble.

She was my soul's mirror, constantly reflecting back to me the truth of who I was inside. How I too had the capacity to be amazed and stirred and inspired by life, to drink up love, to see beyond appearances.

To be free.

18

OM'S CHILDHOOD FARM dog lived seventeen
years, and Sugar was supposed to do the same. She
was supposed to be the flower girl in my wedding
one day, and live to see each member of my family healthy and
happy, which I think is all that Sugar ever wanted. Well, that
and bacon.

I spoke to Julie and Mom almost every day in the weeks
after Sugar's passing. They said the house ached with silence—
they never realized how much they would miss the jingle of
her collar, the shake of her coat. Crumbs stayed on the floor
because our little vacuum cleaner was no longer there, and Julie
hung her collar, which still had white fur on it, on her rearview
mirror along with her high school tassel. Mom had a hard time
sleeping without Sugar curled up next to her, and Julie held on
to Sunny like a life raft when grief swept over her.

I cried with them. I reminisced with them. I told them both
about my upcoming interview at the Humane Society, and
Mom suggested that I bring with me a story I wrote about
Sugar, which turned out to be a spectacular idea. In the end,
that article got me the job.

Even after her death, my sweet girl was still looking after me.

· · ·

THE UNIVERSE MUST have known that I needed a soft landing to break into the world of animal welfare. Had the San Diego Humane Society (SDHS) been your typical shelter with pets crying in cages to the tune of Sarah McLachlan, I doubt I would have been able to handle it.

But SDHS was different because it was a private nonprofit organization rather than a government-run agency, and they had a lot of resources thanks to San Diego's animal-loving community. SDHS cared for dogs, cats, birds, small animals of every kind, horses, and your occasional rooster or reptile. With certified behavior trainers and one of the most advanced shelter medicine teams in the country, animals were rehabilitated and adopted every day. They were never euthanized for space or denied the medical care they needed, no matter how complicated or expensive the procedure. I even read that after orthopedic surgery or neurosurgery, some dogs were treated with acupuncture and physical therapy and walked on state-of-the-art underwater treadmills.

Rather than crowded cages and kennels, adoptable animals stayed in uniquely themed rooms crafted by pro bono interior designers. There was the Paris room and its giant Eiffel Tower scratching post; the library room with its fake fireplace and bookshelves; the Hollywood room with framed photos of Benji and Old Yeller; the New York room with its murals of Central Park and subways; and so on. Inside these "habitats," pets lounged on chew-proof furniture and plush bedding, played with toys, gnawed on Kongs stuffed with treats, and cuddled with volunteers in blue and green vests. They also enjoyed central air, soft rock music, and televisions permanently set to Animal Planet.

Each thoroughly feng-shuied habitat had a glass window where the public could look in and see the animals behaving much like themselves, rather than losing their minds behind steel bars in cages, as they do at most shelters. The atmosphere reduced stress and prevented the spread of disease, but in addition to being very animal friendly, it was also people friendly. The experience of walking through SDHS was designed to be uplifting rather than depressing, which resulted in increased adoptions and a lot more public participation in volunteer and educational programs.

SDHS was just down the road from the police station, ten minutes from a high-end shopping mall, and fifteen minutes from the beach. Each morning, I parked on the street and walked toward a sand-colored building with large archways and a sign that read: "Dedicated to Saving the Life of Every Adoptable Animal." At the entrance, hedges twice my size were pruned into the shapes of cats and dogs. Bright pink, yellow, and red flowers bloomed all around the courtyard, soft rock music played in the background, and water poured into a shallow pool from a hill-shaped fountain, with a statue of a dog chasing a cat on top.

After I picked up a Chocolate Lab Latte from Rocky's café (all proceeds went to the Humane Society), I walked through glass doors into a spacious lobby, where dog- and cat-shaped clouds spanned across high, sky blue ceilings. Everything was sparkly clean, with a lingering odor of disinfectant. To my left, cash registers binged at a retail store more decked out than Petco on Christmas. To my right, a waterfall poured over a bronze wall with the names of donors engraved there.

Plants and water features were scattered about the employee offices. A few large, bright paintings of cats and dogs hung on the wall. And best of all, animals were everywhere. Most of the cubicles had waist-high baby gates attached to them, since employees could bring their pets to work. My favorite office dog was Finley, a three-legged pit bull often curled up beneath a desk in the Education Department. He was rescued from the sadistic world of dogfighting, and he now spent his days visiting children at elementary schools, helping to spread a vital message about compassion and humane treatment toward all living beings. Sometimes I lay on the floor with Finley near his dog bed, and I kissed the stub where his fourth leg should have been.

As marketing coordinator, my role was to promote the adoption of all the animals in our care, and the Humane Society's many programs: Adoptions, Animal Cruelty Investigations, Veterinary Care, Pet-Assisted Therapy, Humane Education, the Animal Rescue Reserve, Behavior and Training, Foster Care, and Volunteer Services.

I wrote animal profiles that were not so different from something you might find on Match.com: the animal's stats (breed, color, sex, weight, adoption fee), plus whether they liked long walks on the beach or chowing down on a bone indoors, whether they couldn't get enough snuggle time or were more independent, et cetera. I posted the profiles on our website along with pictures of the dogs I personally dressed up in bandannas and posed for photographers, attempting to hold them back from lunging at the treats and squeaker toys held over the camera.

I also wrote stories for donor marketing materials and our quarterly magazine, *Animalfare*. I wrote about Janet, a two-month-old puppy who had open-heart surgery. I wrote about Sirius, a two-month-old kitten, and Pumpkin, a Spaniel mix, who were both found on the street with two broken legs. I wrote about a Lab puppy named Manny, on whom we performed six reconstructive surgeries, and Bert and Ernie, two kittens born without eyelids, and on whom we performed corrective surgery. I wrote about our foster program for baby animals, mothers with litters or animals with minor medical needs. I wrote about Mouseberry, a black Chihuahua found on the side of the road with a severe spinal cord injury, who learned to walk again with the help of a red wheelchair. I wrote about four eight-day-old puppies—Nick, Jeff, Drew, and Justin—found outside a dumpster at a Costco and rehabilitated in our care.

Every word I got on the page, whether it was a handful of sentences about an old, diabetic cat or an in-depth article about pit bulls and breed discrimination, filled me up with a sense of purpose and passion I'd never felt before. Sometimes I had the strongest hunch that the moons and planets and stars had convened about what to do with a girl like me, and they came up with the best plan of all, which was to put me here, surrounded by my first love. Dogs.

WHEN I WAS first given keys to the animal habitats, a few weeks after I started working at SDHS, I decided to visit a deceptively calm-looking dog named Maya. A sheet of paper outside her door said that she was a five-year-old blue pit bull with a puppy spirit. I liked puppies—who doesn't like puppies?—and she had cute floppy ears that reminded me of one.

I looked inside the glass window and saw Maya on a pink blanket with her legs sprawled out like a frog, chewing on an already significantly chewed-up squeaker toy. Her coat was not technically blue but a velvety silver, the color of a rain cloud. When I put my key in the door and opened it, Maya charged and pounced on me in an instant, the weight of her body throwing my back against the wall.

"Off!" I said. But that didn't work.

She panted her hot breath in my face. Her claws scratched my arms, and she started doing a down-up dance, four paws on the floor, then two on my shoulders. Four on the floor, then two on my shoulders. I got more scared each time her bearlike paws landed on me, and I heaved a little, like I'd been kicked in the gut. Maya's teeth were so close I could see the yellow stains on them, and for a moment I told myself that this was it: I'd be fired during my first week because I let myself get attacked by a pit bull.

I turned against the wall just to make the sight of her go away, which I'd later learn was very stupid. She jumped on my back, all fifty pounds of her pressing my face to the wall. Somehow I finally squeezed out of the room and shut the door as fast as possible. She kept pouncing, except now against the glass.

Once I caught my breath, I looked around to make sure no one had seen the ridiculousness that had just occurred. Thankfully, my only audience was an elderly dachshund named Delilah and a Boston terrier named Doug, who sat on top of a red couch together across the hall and looked at me with deep concern. I almost felt an urge to explain myself to them, but I reminded myself that they were dogs and I needed to get back to my cubicle to continue pretending like I knew what I was doing. I decided that in the future, tiny poodle mixes were probably more my pace.

BUT AS THE weeks and months went by, it was the pit bulls I was drawn to more than any other breed. Some had energy like Maya and intimidated me, but others, many others, were particularly attentive, sensitive, and affectionate. Smaller dogs were usually grouped in habitats of twos or threes, and they entertained each other, or competed for affection. Since the

rooms were equipped with so many toys, a lot of dogs were far
more interested in getting me to throw a tennis ball or grab on
to the other end of a rope toy than they were in sitting by my
side. And then there were the dogs who ate only when people
were present, so they spent the time I was there chowing down
on their lunch.

But so many of the pit bulls seemed to be singularly focused
on and thrilled about my small presence. They often wanted
nothing more than to cuddle like a lapdog, as if they had no
concept of their size. They tried so hard to fit their big bodies
into my crossed or outstretched legs. When I talked to them
they tilted their wrinkly, boxy heads and perked their ears up
like they were listening.

Sometimes when I felt overwhelmed I held on to their bulky
bodies like an anchor, and I experienced a love that came unexpectedly, a love that bathed me in slobber and acceptance, a
love that was rarely celebrated and often misunderstood. The
pit bulls weren't stingy or picky about their cuddle time. They
never said, *You get ten minutes of my affection and then I'm done
loving you, because I've got other more important things to do.* They
never said, *I can't sit in your lap because of what you did last night,
or an hour ago.*

What they said was: *Is there any possible way I can move this
body of mine closer to you, to sniff your cheek, to know your scent, to
see your eyes?*

19

BBY WAS A brindle four-year-old Staffordshire bull terrier mix who had been in our care for eighteen months and counting. She was a short, hefty girl, weighing in at about sixty pounds. The veterinarians at SDHS had put her on a diet of low-calorie kibble, which Abby was not thrilled about but gobbled up nonetheless.

Prospective adopters often passed by her habitat with little interest. She'd stand on her hind legs at the window, revealing her big tummy and broad chest, cocking her head and balancing along the glass to keep people in her view for as long as possible. When someone made eye contact with her or said a mere word in her direction, her eyes lit up and her long tail whipped around like the blades of a helicopter.

Abby looked more like a combination of bear and hippo, while Sugar could have been easily mistaken for a stuffed animal, but somehow, the two dogs reminded me of each other. Abby gave kisses like there was no tomorrow, and also like Sugar, she loved the great outdoors. She behaved as though the agility yard behind the shelter was the most exciting place on earth. Abby's eyes were always those of a child, pleading five more minutes, begging for more time to explore and play. She sniffed every square inch of that yard and ran in wide laps, perhaps just for the sake of feeling her body and muscles move. As big as she was, she seemed light and even bouncy out there.

One time, she jumped up and took a seat on the concrete bench, surveying the agility yard after ten beautiful minutes of free rein inside it. The sky was mostly white clouds with pockets of vibrant china blue.

"You are Queen of the Astroturf!" I hollered from the other side of the yard.

Her ears moved back and forth like antennas, but she didn't look over at me.

"I'm sorry, you're the Goddess of the Astroturf," I said. Then she turned her beautiful wrinkly face to look over at me, her tail wagging.

PART OF MY job was to bring adoptable animals on various local TV and radio stations. Occasionally, if I was feeling very brave, I brought a cat, kitten, or bunny on camera. But usually, I stuck to the more predictable puppies and dogs.

Things went wrong all the time. There was the dog who wiggled out of his collar and ran loose around the set, nearly knocking over the producer and an expensive camera behind her. The kitten who climbed up my shirt mid-segment, and the other kitten who latched his tiny claws onto the microphone. The dogs who misinterpreted the cameras zooming in on them as large predator eyes, and growled and lunged at them. But in the end, the risk of chaos was worth it if the pet found a home, and after just three to five minutes on air, they almost always did.

During the months Abby had been in our care, I contacted all the newspaper and TV stations we worked with about her, sending pictures, videos, and descriptions that always felt too generic. The handful of adjectives I had in my pocket to describe her (*affectionate, loving, smart, athletic, well-trained, sweet*) just didn't do her justice.

So I had high hopes when I brought her to Channel 8 KFMB for their weekly Pet Friends segment. While a viewer wasn't likely to adopt Abby for her showstopping beauty, they might get to experience the quintessential dog that she was through the screen: all licks and belly rubs, big unapologetic love, and a bottomless appetite for treats and life itself.

When I walked Abby through the doors of the station, she greeted the receptionist as though they were long-lost friends. She sniffed the big-screen TV playing *Dr. Phil*, the coffee tables, and the framed photos of the different news anchors and radio hosts on the wall. Meanwhile, I dug through my blue bag of extra leashes, poop bags, toys, treats, and bandannas ranging in size from tiny to extra large. After debating between a yellow floral print and a glitzy pink bandanna that looked like something Belinda the Good Witch might wear, I chose yellow, so as not to turn off any guys who might be in the market for a big dog.

When the producer said we were up, Abby and I stepped into a long hallway leading to the studio where we'd shoot. She immediately dropped to the floor. Her ears pinned to the back of her head and her tail tucked. Her eyes stayed fixed on the end of the hallway like she was certain we were walking straight into hell.

"What's she so afraid of?" the producer asked.

I shrugged my shoulders and looked around. The lights were bright but nothing too intense. A makeup room to our right carried a strong scent of hairspray, but the break room down the hall smelled like donuts, and I had no idea why Abby wouldn't charge full speed ahead in that direction.

Shannon and a pit bull at the San Diego Humane Society's North County dog park.

ABOVE: Pumpkin, a Chihuahua/Spaniel mix, found on the side of the road with two broken legs. She was rescued by San Diego Humane Society Field Services Officers and made a complete recovery before finding the home of her dreams.

LEFT: Rolo, a young kitten in a playful mood after being bottle-fed at the San Diego Humane Society's Kitten Nursery.

ABOVE: Pit bull puppies posing during a San Diego Humane Society photoshoot.

RIGHT: Peanut, a Sharpei mix who arrived at the San Diego Humane Society at four weeks old, weighing one pound and suffering from pneumonia. He received the 24/7 care he needed to grow into a healthy, spunky pup, and was soon adopted.

Mouseberry, a two-year-old Chihuahua mix found on the side of the road with a severe spinal cord injury. She learned how to walk again with the help of a wheelchair, and was later adopted into a loving family.

Julie, at six years old, holding two-month-old Sugar.
(Courtesy of Kathryn Johnston Gusy.)

Eleanor, an eating disorder survivor, holding Lucy, a survivor of abuse. After Lucy was rehabilitated at the San Diego Humane Society, she lived out her golden years in Eleanor's loving care.

Photo taken by Shannon on the day she and Sweet Pea were reunited at Project Unleashed after the rescue.

Stewie, a ten-month-old poodle mix who beat the odds and continues to inspire many with his resilience and heart. He suffered horrific abuse as a puppy and was rescued by Humane Investigations Officers. After months of veterinary care and rehabilitation, Stewie went on to find the loving home where he thrives today.

Julie (age eight), Sugar (age two), and Shannon (age eleven) on Christmas.
(Courtesy of Kathryn Johnston Gusy.)

Elkie Wills, Director of Community Engagement at the San Diego Humane Society, getting hugs and kisses from Abby, a larger-than-life Staffordshire bull terrier mix.

Shannon greeting a litter of rambunctious puppies at the San Diego Humane Society.

ABOVE: Shannon and two puppies, who were fostered and cared for around-the-clock at the San Diego Humane Society.

RIGHT: Dixie, a survivor of abuse who went on to become an equine therapy horse.

Shannon and Ranger, a fun-loving, twelve-year-old stray shepherd, who helped Sheba, another shepherd at the Humane Society, find the will to live again.

I knew that it would result in an insane amount of gas and maybe even poop on the way home, but she left me no choice. I pulled out the ultimate dog-luring tool from my blue bag: Cheez Whiz.

I lifted up her upper lip and squirted a little bit in her mouth and took a few steps back. She licked her chops and eyed me nervously. Then, like she was in the trenches on some battle-field, she army-crawled a few feet to me and the whiz. I gave her another squirt and stepped back. She crawled another few feet to me, belly rubbing against the carpet. We repeated this all the way down the hall, which took ten long minutes.

When we finally arrived in the studio, Abby froze again. We were already fifteen minutes behind schedule. I asked the producers for a minute and knelt down before her on the shiny wooden floor.

I'd given countless pep talks to dogs before, asking them in all sincerity if they could please not put their butts to the camera or attack the camera or poop or pee or cry and bark. (I never tried talking sense into the cats; all I could do was pray for the best.) Cheesy drool hung from Abby's lips and she gazed at the camera equipment and a small stage lit up by floodlights behind me.

"Abby," I said, in an upbeat, soothing voice, "I'm not sure what you are so afraid of, but this is a good thing and everyone here loves you. You're a good girl, you're my goddess girl."

She inched her muzzle closer to my knee in a hopeless effort to hide behind it. I stroked the top of her head and massaged the layers of skin on the back of her neck.

"Abby, sometimes the best things come from doing what scares you," I said.

Then I kissed her stinky lips, her nose, her ears, and in be-tween her big eyes. I stood up and called her name, giving her leash another gentle pull.

Her eyebrows raised and she sighed a deep breath, and then, ever so slowly, she followed. She army-crawled her way behind me all the way to the stage. Upon her arrival, everyone in the studio cheered, but quietly, so as not to spook her again. I gave Abby a piece of rawhide, which she mindlessly chomped on for the next three minutes. It soothed her like a pacifier to a baby.

The anchor across from me was a handsome man in his forties with black gelled hair and dressed in a suit. He referred to Abby as "full-figured," and I told San Diego that despite her bulky appearance, she was a gentle and affectionate soul looking for a family to love. I reached down every now and then to stroke that silly, nervous goddess at my feet.

And soon enough, Abby found her home.

OUR FEARS MAY not always be rational, but that doesn't make them any less real. I never figured out exactly why Abby was so scared at the studio, but the reasons usually don't matter anyway.

A terrier-poodle mix I'd later adopt, Bella, had a mortal fear of flies and human sneezing (dog sneezes didn't bother her). If a single fly was in the house, she flattened herself like a pancake and crawled under the couch, trembling as though the fly were some vicious monster and she was its prey. Whenever someone took a deep inhale before a sneeze, she took cover under the couch, too. Sometimes it would take us hours to lure her out, and unlike with Abby, Cheez Whiz didn't do us any good.

Sometimes I laughed, but it never once annoyed me. I didn't even care when we had to miss a grooming appointment after a fly touched down on Bella's nose, traumatic enough to keep her under the couch for eight hours. I knew what it was like to be terrified of something that people just didn't understand.

Like being left alone with a fridge full of food. Like not fitting into your skinny jeans after a big meal. Like your own reflection in the mirror.

All the while I worked at the San Diego Humane Society, I never lost my fear of "getting fat." I felt uncomfortable in my body, even though I was finally nourishing it properly on a daily basis. On an intellectual level, I knew that getting fat was a stupid thing to fear, especially when there were children who feared for their lives all across the world and parents who feared they wouldn't be able to put food on the table and soldiers who feared they would never return home from war.

But fear doesn't care about reasonability or rationality or even sanity. It cares about swallowing you whole.

20

STEWIE, A NINE-MONTH-OLD, ten-pound miniature poodle mix, was thrown into a tub of scorching hot water by his owners and then left to suffer from his wounds. When our Humane Investigations officers found him, he was covered in second- and third-degree burns, as well as a resistant bacterial infection. Veterinarians performed a cutting-edge treatment commonly used in human medicine for burn victims, which involved removing some of Stewie's blood, spinning it down in a special centrifuge, collecting the platelet-rich portion of the blood, and applying it to the wounds.

The treatment was successful, though as a result of what he'd endured, Stewie would never look like a normal dog. He had hair on his face and legs, but the center of his body would forever remain a sheet of raw, red skin, sensitive to touch and prone to injury. A permanent reminder of his suffering.

Just like with people, trauma from physical and emotional abuse can stay with dogs, sometimes in ways that aren't immediately visible to the eye. I once met a bullmastiff named Romeo who was an affectionate pile of mush around women but lunged and snapped at any man he saw. He'd been abused years earlier by a man, and despite all the work our trainers did with him to undo that hurt, Romeo simply could not forget his past. After several weeks of unsuccessful rehabilitation, the decision was made to euthanize him.

While I understood that he was unsafe to place back into the community, another part of me knew that sometimes the body responds to yesterday's scars before we have the chance to think about it, to choose our behaviors. The sound of my father's voice once made me punch a wall and bruise my knuckles, and another time the mere sight of a toilet made me cry. But I do neither of those things today.

Studies show that abused dogs can recover by learning to make new associations to replace negative ones; that dogs are intelligent and emotional beings. I couldn't help but wonder, were we expecting Romeo to heal from a wound in weeks that would take most humans many years? Had we labeled him *too far gone* before he ever had the chance to come back? To make different choices?

Sometimes, we give up on healing, for ourselves and for others, too soon. And on the day I watched Romeo's strong black legs and long, wagging tail follow a female caregiver into the euthanasia room, I wept like he was my own.

AFTER THE BRUTALITY Stewie faced so early in life, he would have had every reason to fear people. Yet miraculously, he remained a sweet and loving dog. He wasn't very calm and self-assured, but I wouldn't be, either, if someone who was supposed to care for me threw me into a tub of boiling water.

Sometimes Stewie ran in manic circles and barked like crazy out of the blue. He was occasionally convinced that another dog was staring him down, when it was really just Stewie's reflection in a window. He often winced and became nervous around loud noises. But in the end, Stewie was still as affectionate as ever, and isn't that what really counts? Who cares about a little nuttiness when we live with open hearts?

One veterinarian told me that in the beginning, when they were still not sure if he would survive the burns, Stewie squirmed to the front of his cage every time he saw a vet tech approaching. Even the slightest movement caused him pain, and usually a vet was coming to change his bandages or give him an injection, but still, he drew closer to them, laying his small head in their white-gloved hands as one might lie on a pillow.

Post-surgery, Stewie required months of around-the-clock care from our veterinarians. I followed him around with a video camera to capture his long road to recovery, and I tried very hard not to create even the slightest discomfort for him. When I brought him outside to the agility yard, I put sunscreen over every inch of his tender skin. Stewie loved to play fetch, but I paused after every few throws to give him water, tilting a blue plastic bowl to his lips. Sometimes his skin cracked and bled from running too hard, and I'd sweep him up into my arms and sprint to the vet department so that they could apply more ointment and bandages. As a member of the species that committed such unthinkable cruelty against Stewie, I wanted to do everything I could to make him feel safe.

Stewie wasn't always on his best behavior, but honestly, he could have taken a dump in my favorite purse and I wouldn't have said a word. He lifted his leg to pee on me. He pulled at my hair and my shoelaces. He jumped all over my legs. But there was nothing he could ever do to make me call him a bad dog. For the rest of his days, all I wanted Stewie to experience was gentleness and love.

So I told him he was a good dog as often as I could. I

celebrated him when he made little behavioral improvements, like sitting calmly instead of jumping around like a maniac. I told him he was the champion of my heart. I treated him like he was the most beautiful, precious little nutcase on the planet, because really, he was.

If I could have adopted just an ounce of that loving and compassionate attitude toward my own self, I doubt I would have ever relapsed back into bulimia.

But after about a year working at SDHS, I did.

The relapse felt sudden and unexpected, but looking back, I can see that the way I treated animals like Stewie bore no resemblance to how I treated myself.

If I made a single mistake at work, voices in my head were punishing me all day about it. If I had a headache or a migraine, I didn't go outside for a breath of fresh air—I popped another Advil and worked hard enough to forget about it. When my body ached from handling big dogs, or my mind was stressed to the brink, I pushed harder.

Dad would sometimes call me and leave drunk messages, and I played and replayed them as a form of torture. But I secretly believed the exact same thing that I did when I was seventeen: Grieving him was weak. Grieving him was stupid. Grieving him was wrong. He wasn't dead yet, and in fact, during one period of sobriety, ninety days I think, he held my hands and made amends to me in a church basement, crying sober tears about the pain he'd caused.

"Remember how it used to be the two of us? Remember how close we were?" he asked.

I told him that of course I did. I told him that I would always love him, and that I missed him, and that I wanted him back in my life.

Then he got drunk, and when Mom called me to tell me so, I swallowed down a lump of tears and called myself stupid for expecting anything different

Stupid. Brilliant. Fat. Thin. Bad. Good.—I didn't know that my existence could never be summed up by a label. My thoughts were so loud and all-consuming and deeply ingrained that I misperceived them as Truth. They blinded me to the fact that like Stewie, I too was a resilient animal being. I too had the remarkable and mysterious capacity for love.

In favor of helping as many dogs as possible at SDHS, I often neglected my own needs. I stopped seeing a nutritionist and preparing three meals and three snacks a day, and I went to therapy less and less. That roomy sense of time had faded, and I rushed around fueled by a thousand things to do. I told myself I was running myself ragged for the animals, but the deeper truth was that I was still living to matter in the eyes of others, to be seen, to be told I was good. My God was whatever you thought of me.

Inevitably, there were days I'd come home exhausted and stressed and resentful. I'd check out by watching mindless television and having a few glasses of wine. I'd go on Facebook and get jealous of people who seemed so happy and carefree and put together all the time.

On one of these exhausted/stressed/resentful nights, I ate a big dinner in the apartment while watching a *Sex and the City* marathon. Danny was working late. I felt uncomfortably full, and a thought arose as casually as a reminder to pick up the dry cleaning. It said, "Just throw up, it's no big deal."

If I did not have such a history with addiction, my mind might have located all of its memories about how throwing up *was* in fact a big deal for me, landing me at Rosewood not so long ago. But addictive craving bypasses all knowledge of past experience and consequences. It puts you in a truth blackout, and your wisdom and sanity disappear.

And so just like that, I paused *Sex and the City* and went to the bathroom and puked.

And then a few nights later, I puked again.

And then a few nights after that.

In the beginning, Danny tried to be patient and supportive. Both of us thought it was just a setback because I had been doing so well. We were sure I'd work out what happened in therapy and return to healthy eating soon.

Danny treated the situation like he did sports. He had a game plan for me to get better, and he encouraged me to face the opponent head-on. Danny gave me pep talks and tried to pump me up. Together, we taped my meal plan to the fridge. We bought scales and measuring cups so that I could weigh and measure my food as I did at Rosewood. Danny went to a group for family members of loved ones suffering from eating disorders, and I got back into weekly therapy.

But as much as Danny wanted me to get better, and as much as I wanted to get better for him, some sick part of me craved the relief that came of filling up and getting empty, no matter how destructive it was. Like a spiderweb, addiction catches both prey and beautiful light. It simultaneously kills and glistens.

TWO MONTHS AFTER I relapsed, Danny came home from work one day to find a war zone of wrappers and crumbs and melted ice cream in our kitchen, and me on my knees in front of the toilet bowl, wiping my mouth with one hand and flushing with the other. I had tried to kick the bathroom door closed, but he blocked it with his hand. He stood in the doorway in his business suit and clenched his eyes shut for two or three seconds, like he couldn't stomach the sight of me. Then he turned around and walked into the living room.

"I can't believe you," he said, and I sat back on my knees and dropped my face into my reeking palms. I couldn't believe me. And I couldn't imagine how he could ever look at me the same again. I was wearing his T-shirt and sweatpants. A glob of peanut butter was stuck to my wrist. Some of the vomit had splashed off the toilet seat and onto the floor beside me. I cleaned it up with some toilet paper and flushed again. Then I washed my hands profusely, staring at the silver faucet, unable to face myself in the mirror.

WHEN I STEPPED out of the bathroom, Danny sat on our couch with his face in his hands. He'd taken off his jacket and wore black dress pants and a lavender shirt. He was an extremely clean person, and the apartment looked like a pack of dogs had torn through all the food and dragged it everywhere.

I wanted so badly to undo what Danny was seeing, to rewind back to an hour ago, or even better—two months ago—and make myself do the right thing, which would have been to never start bingeing and puking again in the first place.

"I'm sorry," I said and sat beside him on the couch. The air thinned between us. I grabbed both of his hands. I swayed back and forth, sobbing and begging him not to leave me.

He shook his head and said that he loved me but he didn't know how to help me anymore. Maybe my living with him and depending on him was making it worse. He couldn't understand why I kept repeating the behaviors that made me so miserable. "Why do you keep doing this?" he asked, his eyes more sad than angry.

I didn't have an explanation for him. Just more hysterical pleas and promises. I said I couldn't imagine ever being happy without him. I said I'd try harder. I'd get it together. I'd never do this again.

Danny wouldn't look at me while I talked. Then he finally moved his gaze from the food all over the counter to me, waiting until I calmed down, until my sobbing and trembling subsided. He squeezed my hands tight.

"I love you. But I love myself, too," he said. "And I'm not going to live with someone who does this to herself."

He released his grip. Then he let me go.

21

D ANNY MOVED FORTY-FIVE minutes away, and I
moved into a studio in Ocean Beach, just a few miles
from the Humane Society.

I told family and friends that the reason for our separation
was that I'd never lived on my own before, and I wanted to
experience it before we got married. In reality, marriage was
the furthest thing from our minds. Danny was busy distancing
himself from me, and I was busy distancing myself from health.
We still talked every day, and we were not seeing other people,
but there was an inescapable tension between us. I could see in
his eyes how much he didn't trust me. And of course, I hadn't
given him much reason to.

Almost nothing mattered anymore. Recklessness lodged
itself into the channels of my mind. One day, I almost crashed
my car and got a ticket, running through a red light on my
way to the grocery store. I often threw up in the dumpster
behind my complex, where hipster addicts liked to hang out.
I carried around lozenges for my perpetually sore throat,
Visine for my bloodshot eyes, and paper towels in my car
to clean up after vomiting. I also carried around a photo of
Julie in my back pocket—she was my diver's suit in this cold

ocean, my goose-bump-covered skin, and inside me like the smoothest pulse. I wanted her face to keep me from going off the deep end. But it didn't.

At least two or three times a week for the next three months, I woke up surrounded by fast-food, cake, and cookie wrappers in my studio apartment. I devoured more food and puked my guts out more often than ever before, sometimes up to twenty times a night. Occasionally, I vomited blood.

I kept telling myself that I was just having a bad day, a bad month. I was going to get back on track tomorrow. Straight out of bed. First fucking thing. Tomorrow.

The alternative to flimsy promises about tomorrow would have been to throw up my hands and admit that I didn't know where I'd be tomorrow, or if I'd ever find my way back to health. But acknowledging that was far too scary. Letting go and falling into the great unknown seemed riskier than another round of cheeseburgers. And again and again, another round of cheeseburgers it was.

Had I not been working at SDHS at the time, it would have been nearly impossible to wake up the next morning, get dressed, and leave my sunlit studio, which was in fact very depressing. Sometimes, when the room was filled with morning light, the glint of a crumpled burger wrapper on the floor flashed in my face and shame gripped my heart and I threw the covers over my head, wanting to sleep forever. But then the thought of a shelter dog—a distinct face and story—would rouse me out of bed.

BEFORE I WENT to my desk, I howled and cried and cussed and grabbed at the ends of my hair in the dog habitats. I told homeless pit bulls and shepherds and Chihuahuas about what a piece of shit I was. I said I wanted to die. I said I was a liar and a failure and was fat and a monster. I hunched over their stringy, matted fur. I stared into their honest eyes. I let their unclean tongues cover my face. I never wanted to leave them, even if they smelled bad or barked enough to give me a headache. The safest place I could be was by their side.

During a time when I felt like no one could see the real me—not even myself—I felt profoundly seen by the shelter dogs. Their attentive eyes and steady tail wags told me that I still mattered to someone. They gave me a level of comfort and acceptance and adoration that I was certain I didn't deserve.

ONE MORNING, AFTER a particularly rough night throwing up Kit Kat bars and burritos, I walked into a habitat painted lime green with a glow-in-the-dark full moon on the wall, a sort of space-age theme. Angel was sprawled across a green couch, gnawing on a bone. She was a white, heavyset pit bull with a head twice the size of mine and a wrinkly snow-powder face, with a touch of pink around the eyes and nose. Angel came to the shelter after being hit by a car, and now one front leg was slightly shorter than the other. When she walked, she had an adorable strut, an irresistible wiggle, and a butt so big and no-ticeable I nicknamed her Kim K.

The instant Angel saw me she leapt off the couch and jumped up on her hind legs, balancing so we were almost at eye level looking at each other through the glass. She barked at the prospect of my arrival, and I mouthed, "Shh, girl. Sit, sit down."

We were supposed to wait until the dogs calmed and sat before we entered their room, so as to promote good behavior.

But I could barely train myself to get up in the morning, so I wasn't very consistent with the dogs.

After about a minute of nonstop barking, Angel's butt finally hit the floor for about a millisecond, probably by accident, but it was good enough for me. I opened the door and got on my knees to give Angel a hug. She came barreling into me, her whole backside wagging along with her tail. I wrapped my arms around her. I felt the strength of her seventy-pound body. I smelled the stench of her Milk-Bone breath. I looked into her bright amber eyes and said, "How's my sweet girl?"

Angel was the kind of dog who would try to kiss a bee or a lion or a fire-breathing dragon, not because she was unintelligent but because she just loved to kiss that much. So I sat down on the linoleum floor and let her kiss my face. Then I leaned back against the wall and Angel climbed into my lap (only the front half of her body fit). She rolled over, belly to the ceiling, and gazed up at me. She stretched her paws in the air as if to expand her stomach so that there was more of it for me to pet. When I petted her near her hind legs, she kicked them around like she was ticklish. When I stroked her behind the crease of her soft, white ears, she leaned into my hand.

At one point, I sneezed, probably due to dog hair up my nose, and Angel lifted her head from my lap to look up at me. How wide open and glistening her eyes were, how free and alive! There was no past or future, no stories of shame inside them.

So many stories lived behind my eyes. I carried the people I hurt, the lies I told, my sick relationship with food, wherever I went. My mind was rarely grounded in the moment. My past was heavy and constant; my thoughts wouldn't leave me alone.

But when I was with the shelter dogs, I didn't have anything to hide. Sometimes what existed behind my eyes fell away. I wasn't *bulimic* or *unlovable* or *fat* or a *liar*. I was a part of life again. I was an observer, and to more than just the dark cyclical patterns of my mind—here was the strong, sturdy presence of another—the breath moving in and out of Angel's chest, the beating of her heart, the force of life moving through her and through me.

22

SOMETIMES ON MY lunch breaks at SDHS, I went to an eating disorder recovery group. The meetings took place in an old, one-story office building next door to a senior citizens' club bustling with bingo players. Across the street, men bench-pressed in wife-beaters at a garage-style gym, and nearby, a few low-rider cars were parked in front of a medical marijuana shop.

One Tuesday afternoon, I got to the meeting late, smelling faintly of dog poop and covered in husky hair. My own hair was a hot mess, since a pit bull puppy had mistaken my ponytail for a rope toy an hour earlier.

Inside a room with blue carpet, I took a seat in the circle of metal chairs. Prayers and a few poems were taped to the white walls around me. The marijuana smell lingered and the ground vibrated from hip-hop music at the gym. About twenty people were gathered, and most wore black, the so-called best color to hide your fat behind, real or perceived. Beside me sat a yoga teacher who looked like Reese Witherspoon. Beside her, an old, three-hundred-pound woman in a wheelchair. Beside her, an overweight, proud grandpa who barely fit in his seat and needed a cane to walk. Beside him, a college student who covered her entire face with a tissue as if it were a warm towel, and wept quietly.

There were no popular kids or band geeks or jocks here, no walls of separation. Anorexics sat next to the thing they most feared, fat people. Fat people sat next to exercise bulimics who spent half their lives on treadmills. Christians next to atheists. Virgins next to sex addicts. It didn't matter. We were all here for one reason, and the reason was simple: we were addicts and we were dying.

We ranged in age from our late teens to our late eighties. We were not the kind of people who ate a pint of ice cream after a bad breakup, felt some self-loathing, then went back to eating normally the next day. We were the people who used ice cream like a knife to tear ourselves apart. We weren't the kind of people who dabbled in anorexia, bulimia, or binge eating in our teenage years, then got some therapeutic help and moved on. Weight Watchers, gastric bypass, personal training, and diets didn't work for us. We were the ones who lost teeth while vomiting. We were the ones who relapsed the day after we got out of rehab. We were the ones who had all the knowledge in the world about our condition, but couldn't apply it. We were the ones who got lap bands and burst them.

The meeting started and a woman in her seventies with red hair and a thick New York accent shared her story.

"My husband has dementia and every day, I'm a good girl. I go to work and then I go visit with him and he cries every time I leave and I promise I'll come back tomorrow and I do."

She tugged on a black earring. "I always do, but you know what? I eat. I eat all night. I eat the way he cries, uncontrollably and endlessly. I just . . . I really need God's help."

She looked across the room and into my eyes when she said those words, and I stared down at the floor. I thought she was talking about a conventional concept of God, and I had no interest in the God I was brought up to believe in, the one who made my father weep for his sins and told gay people they couldn't love each other and women what to do with their bodies. I didn't realize that a spiritual experience didn't necessarily have to happen at a church or a temple, and that no burning bush was required.

Never in a million years did I think that a person like me could have a spiritual experience, let alone at an animal shelter. But in time, as the narrow lens of my awareness expanded to include the genuine concern of others, mostly four-legged, I'd gradually awaken to the truth every religion points to: love makes all things possible.

23

SOMETIMES, DESPITE YOUR stubbornness, peace chooses you. Sometimes, despite your track record, you find a well of strength inside. That happened to me one Saturday morning, five months into what I'd later call "the relapse from hell," when I woke up and decided to go to the beach.

I hadn't slept most of the night because Danny's arms weren't wrapped around me and I feared they never would be again. My stomach growled for food and my mind craved a breakfast burrito and my heart desperately longed to know that I could eat it and keep it down.

So I changed into my yoga pants and Danny's old T-shirt, and I grabbed my keys and wallet. I stopped at a Mexican drive-thru and got an egg-and-cheese burrito wrapped in foil. Then I drove to La Jolla Cove.

On a cliff overlooking the water, gulls and pelicans flew overhead, and a plastic bag belly-danced in the wind. Rose petals scattered on a nearby beach, the remains of a wedding. Tall palms loomed over me, and the only people around were surfers and divers, who were already in the water. Perhaps sixty feet below me, on a cluster of rocks rooted into the ocean's floor, dozens of sea lions and harbor seals gathered to sunbathe.

There was a chill in the air and a potent smell of dead fish, and I wrapped a towel around my arms. The golden-brown sea lions, with their broad chests and big front flippers, seemed to get around more easily on the rocks than the seals, who were smaller and squirmed like caterpillars. They moved so differently on land than in water: effortless, underwater dancing versus a perpetual state of flopping and wiggling. Every foot appeared to take so much effort, but nobody, not even the largest seals, seemed to mind. These animals were like the rest of nature. A strand of grass never throws a temper tantrum when it gets dried out by the sun or shat upon by a Saint Bernard. A flower doesn't look at winter and refuse it to come. It wilts, peacefully.

Once the seals found a spot to their liking on the rocks, many sat completely still, arching their necks and heads toward the sun. I stared out at the sun, too, mesmerized by its beams of light across the water, and how it made the seals glisten on land. For a few minutes, I focused on the beauty around me rather than the hot, greasy food in my lap. And then I took a deep breath and unwrapped the breakfast burrito.

I shut my eyes and took a bite. And then another. And then another. When I wanted to look down at my stomach, I looked out at the ocean. When voices in my mind whispered about how I should get into my car and find a place to puke, I listened harder to the crashing waves.

I finished the burrito and stayed with the sun and the seals and sea lions for about an hour that morning, feeling the fullness inside me, and letting it be.

When I stood up to leave, I caught sight of one small silver seal, at least half of the size of the others. She pushed off from nothing solid, just an oncoming wave, and flung herself onto a large, mossy rock. She squirmed her way at least six feet to the top of the rock and sat up tall, her wet, shining chest to the sky.

Then she threw her neck back and adjusted her head an inch or two, it seemed, so that she could face the sun most directly.

What a conscious choice that seemed to be! What an effort! I almost felt like applauding.

Then I thought about the little effort I'd made that day, to get to this beach and eat breakfast.

It was great effort, actually.

And for some of us, that is what recovery from addiction takes.

Little, great, conscious efforts.

When I got into my car and drove home from the beach that morning, I thought that maybe this was the end of it. I was done. I was finally breaking ties with this terrible disease.

And at just the thought, a feeling of warmth washed over my entire body, as if just like the seals, I was directly facing the sun.

24

LUCY WAS A thirteen-year-old wire-haired Jack Russell terrier whom I met a few months before the relapse from hell began. The details of the abuse Lucy survived were not clear, but she came to us with chemical burns on her head and BB gun pellets buried beneath her skin. Most of the hair on her scalp and face had burned off completely. A thick, squiggly line of pink skin stretched from the top of her head down in between her eyes to her muzzle. A veiny red sac bulged at the side of her right eye, making it look like it was about to fall out of its socket at any moment. At first I couldn't look at Lucy without flinching.

But in a short time, I went from not being able to look directly at Lucy to being fascinated by her. All the other dogs at SDHS typically wanted something with urgency, whether it be to eat or play or go outside or cuddle. But Lucy was different. There wasn't a twinge of neediness in her eyes. She was so peaceful all the time, as if she had been through enough in life and nothing could unsettle her now. She seemed an old soul, and I came to think of her as the canine version of Buddha, the joyous one with hands outstretched to the sky and a big, round tummy.

One day in the play yard, we sat down in the fake grass enclosed by barbed-wire fence. It was such a warm and sunny day that the air itself seemed pale yellow. Nearby, a small agility obstacle course gleamed in the sunlight beside two plastic gray chests full of dog bones, balls, chew toys, and squeakers.

I loved taking dogs to the play yard for the simple fact that they never looked up at me and asked, *May I run laps here? May I sniff this nifty grass? May I sunbathe? May I pick up this stuffed raccoon toy and squeak the hell out of it?*

Lucy loved to cuddle in the sun, so she sat in my lap while I stroked her stringy reddish-bronze fur. She was plump in the center of her body, skinny in the limbs—a short but compact little dog. Usually when we sat together, Lucy watched the world around us attentively. She'd observe a small bird swoop down and pick up a dog treat crumb with her beak, then fly away and perch herself on the branch of a billowing tree. She'd watch the thick bushes shake in the wind. At times, she'd arch her head back and sniff the air, as if catching the scent of the sky.

But on this day, Lucy focused all her attention on me. I checked to see if I had any treats in my pockets to spark her interest, but I didn't. I waited for Lucy to glance left or right, but she just kept facing me in my lap and staring up into my eyes, as though she could see through them.

It was as if she were saying, *There is nothing you can do to make me look away.*

I HAD CONSIDERED adopting Lucy myself, but I knew it wasn't the right time. I wanted Lucy to be adopted by someone who could make up for the story of violence on her skin. I wanted her to be paid great attention to and spoiled rotten. I wanted her to sleep in a plush bed at night and sunbathe in a yard during the day. I wanted her to be loved madly during the last years of her life. Though I knew I'd love her madly, I was afraid I wouldn't be able to give her the attention she deserved.

So I got about the business of trying to find her the right home, bringing Lucy on television and posting her picture in the paper.

And that's when Eleanor came along, a strong and kind eighty-three-year-old woman who saw Lucy's photo in the *Union-Tribune* one Sunday morning. Eleanor had recently lost her husband and her black Lab.

"I wanted to adopt a dog who was as old and resilient as me," she later said. "And I knew that dog was Lucy when I saw her face."

After Eleanor adopted Lucy, I interviewed her for a story a few times, and we became friends. Eleanor lived in a small home with a roommate who worked at a bookstore, just a few blocks away from San Diego State University. Each time I came over, Eleanor offered me fresh vegetables from her garden and a book from the shelf she kept on her front porch for passersby to take.

A week or so after my peaceful morning with the seals, during which I sadly found out that I was not done with bulimia (or perhaps more accurately, it wasn't done with me), I drove over to Eleanor's house. We sat on a couch covered in quilted blankets in her small living room. Outside the window, rush-hour traffic built up on the road and the sun beat down hard on the front lawn, which was mostly gravel and dead grass. Lucy curled up nose-to-tail on a pillow in between us and looked much healthier than she had at SDHS. Eleanor said this was mostly due to her Reiki sessions (Lucy's that is), as well as two eye surgeries and lots of TLC. The two of them rarely spent a moment apart. It was exactly the sort of home I hoped Lucy would find.

For the next hour, Eleanor and I sipped chamomile tea and talked about animals. Eleanor told me they were the "glue" of her life, a source of comfort and connection from the very beginning. She opened up to me about how life hadn't been easy for her when she was young. Eleanor grew up with an alcoholic father and brother, and she struggled with an eating disorder in her twenties.

"What kind of eating disorder?" I asked, a little too quickly.

Eleanor pushed a strand of white hair out of her blue eyes and reached down with her pale hand to touch Lucy's head.

"Anorexia," she said. "And just an overall fear of food."

Lucy rolled onto Eleanor's lap and she scratched her tummy. Then she told me about her first diet as a teenager. What began as a desire to be thin then took on a destructive momentum that she couldn't stop. When she was my age, she lived in New York City and worked at a bookstore where celebrities often hung out. She never considered her body thin enough and spent hours obsessing over recipe books and staring at images of wholesome meals she never allowed herself to have. In the end, Eleanor was admitted to a mental hospital and began working with a therapist who would eventually write a chapter of a book based on a question that Eleanor asked. The question was, "What do you mean by love?"

"I just didn't know what love was or where it came from anymore. All I knew was that I wanted to be thinner," Eleanor said.

Amen, sister, is what I wanted to say, but instead, I just nodded and told her that I understood. As if I didn't have eight years of intimate experience with this subject. As if some part of me didn't still believe that love and a thin body were absolutely interchangeable.

Before I left Eleanor's house that day, she said, "I wish that when you're young you could have the wisdom of having lived many years. Because by the time you are my age, you look back at how you hated your body, when really, it's been your only constant companion on earth. And a good one at that."

I nodded again, unable to meet Eleanor's eyes, reaching over to pet Lucy. She lifted her chin from her paws to blink up at me, the soft weight of her body pressing against my hand.

25

THE NEXT DAY, I visited my favorite dog, Buster, a German shepherd with a soft gold coat and two stiff legs that made him wobble when he walked. Humane Investigations officers had found Buster injured and malnourished, limping around a backyard.

Buster was like a ninety-five-year-old man in a four-year-old canine body. Sometimes he stood up successfully, but often he fell in the process of trying to balance his weight on his unsteady legs, as if all of his bones and muscles gave out at once. Buster's back was usually hunched over and his hips were crooked, but his spirit was that of a puppy, full of curiosity and eagerness. Sometimes when he panted, he revealed a toothy overbite, which made him look like he was smiling.

I sat with Buster in the Hollywood Room, where pictures of Benji, Lassie, and Rin Tin Tin covered the walls, along with bright gold stars. It was almost time for me to get back to my desk and begin another game of pretend, but I wanted to soak up every last minute of comfort in Buster's animal presence. For as long as possible, I wanted to be with someone who wouldn't comment on how tired I looked or ask what I did last night, which was a lot of wasting money on junk food and puking and crying.

Buster laid his head down on my outstretched legs, and for a few minutes, I gently stroked him on his chest and behind his neck. He sighed and then I did, too. A wave of exhaustion came over me. I'd slept maybe four hours.

I'm not sure how long I drifted off into the dark space of my mind, but soon enough, I imagined myself standing on the edge at Sunset Cliffs, a place near my studio where several people had fallen to their death over the years.

The people I loved the most were waiting in a line, a safe distance away. My mother came up and hugged me and told me that she loved me, then she turned and walked away. Then came my sister. Then Danny. Then Dad. When they left me, I knew I'd never see them again. I apologized. I said I'd tried as hard as I could, but I couldn't try anymore. They took heavy steps away from the ledge, but they didn't cry or try to plead with me. They all seemed to know what I had decided, and that their love couldn't save me. No one's love could.

Buster struggling to his feet interrupted my thoughts. I got onto my knees and held out my arms in case he fell, but Buster stood taller and sturdier than I'd seen before. His face was eye-level with me, his back almost completely straightened. I moved my hands from his sides and set them down on my lap. Buster then leaned his body forward, and in what felt like a conscious and gentle effort, he pressed his nose into the center of my chest, as if in encouragement for me to embrace him.

I don't know if I'll ever be able to explain how when I wrapped my arms around Buster's young and old body, I felt like I was holding on to myself: not the self who was thin or fat, good or bad, filled to the brim with hope or suicidal; not the one who'd never be okay and didn't deserve to be. I held on to where strength and vulnerability lived in close quarters, where the capacity for great sadness and joy flowed in my bloodstream, where my humanity was a fabric of many threads, each of them unique and even beautiful.

With the sound of Buster's bushy tail thudding against the starry wall, my body and my mind softened. I reached my hands on either side of him and massaged my fingers deep into his flanks, breathing in the grassy scent of his coat. I thought about how I never chose to love dogs. I was just born loving them, and now here I was, surrounded by countless pairs of soulful eyes and wagging tails helping me to survive.

Buster's legs quivered and he lay down, collapsing into my lap. I leaned over to kiss his bony head and then stroked his golden fur along his back, which came out in clumps and floated in the air around us.

There was much to do at SDHS. We had just wrapped up our big fund-raising event, the Fur Ball, and I needed to write a story on it. My coworkers, two of whom were my closest friends, had been frustrated with me lately. They couldn't depend on me as they did when I first joined the marketing team. I often got to work late and misplaced files and lost the keys I needed to get into animal habitats. I couldn't concentrate for long periods of time, and I showed up in heels and a business suit on days I was meant to be handling dogs, and then in sneakers and jeans on days when I was supposed to be dressed nicely for an important meeting. I even left my cell phone unattended in a dog habitat with an eight-week-old pit bull puppy, who ate its black case. She had to get her stomach pumped and spend the night in Medical.

I didn't want to keep letting people and animals down. But I also didn't want to keep letting myself down.

When I walked out of Buster's habitat, I knew what I had to do. I knew I needed to get some help, and not first thing tomorrow, but right now.

I turned around and looked back at him through the window. He sprawled his tired bones across the blanket of my pride and looked back at me with honest, brown eyes, tilting his head as if to say, *You'll have to move me if you want this back.*

I TOLD MY boss that I was sick and then drove to a recovery meeting, where I cried for almost the whole hour. Even though it was embarrassing, I just couldn't get hold of myself. When I looked down and saw Buster's gold hair on my pants, it was as though the fleshy pieces of my heart came pouring out of my eyes. People gave me soft, compassionate glances and handed me Kleenexes.

When the time came for us all to gather in a circle and pray, nothing in my body resisted or felt tight, as it usually did. The words came off my tongue slowly and carefully, with all the sincerity and humility I could muster.

When I opened my eyes and my hands were released, I raised one of them high and nearly shouted like my life was on the line, which it was: "Is anybody here going to lunch?"

A man with white hair, flushed cheeks, and a potbelly came up to me, and a woman in her late seventies who I always thought was off her rocker. Tom was a saxophone player earning his degree to be a psychologist. Claire was a suicide attempt survivor, "over that nonsense now." She said she was in love with a man for the first time in her life, though she'd had husbands before.

We ate lunch together at a restaurant down the street, which was almost exclusively the color pink and adorned with fake gold. After I finished a bowl of lentil soup and a Greek salad, I promised that I would call one of them that night during dinner.

I returned to my beach studio and slept for a few hours. When I woke up, I called Claire. I ate a peanut butter sandwich while on the phone with her. She sat there telling me to be brave, listening to me chew.

My mind had its ideas about what kind of a person needs support eating peanut butter.

But then my heart said, *You do, dear girl*. And I held the phone closer.

SOMETIMES WE TAKE leaps of faith, and sometimes we take tiny steps. Even the tiniest step can require a lot of courage. Like climbing out of denial and admitting my real need for help. Like trusting someone who said I wouldn't die from eating a bowl of pasta, and taking another bite. Like reaching for a pen or a yoga mat when what I really wanted to do was reach for a cookie. Like searching for a smile in my heart when my mind was busy screaming about how sad and serious I should be.

The world is not what made me so sick and miserable—it was my way of seeing myself in the world. If I was going to have a healthy relationship with food again, I needed to learn how to take care of myself. I'd always known this on an intellectual level, but that wisdom had finally dropped down to my heart—where it really counts.

What I needed wasn't a new body but a new set of eyes. I needed to come to regard my own self with the same kind of tolerance and love I naturally extended toward all animals.

So that when I looked at my arms, I saw how many people and animals they'd held, rather than a need to tone them at the gym.

And when I looked at my legs, I didn't see fat thighs, but how far they'd carried me in this life.

And when I looked at my throat, I saw a gateway to speaking my truth, rather than a vessel for getting empty.

And when I looked at the big mistakes my mind said should never have happened, like six months of godawful bingeing and puking, I could see how my suffering was the birthplace of something beautiful. Compassion.

PART
THREE

"Until one has loved an animal,
a part of one's soul remains unawakened."

—ANATOLE FRANCE

26

SHEBA WAS A ten-year-old shepherd mix who seemed like she had given up on life when she walked through the doors of the San Diego Humane Society.

There was something graceful and dignified about her, even when she was afraid. She had the tallest, perkiest ears, black around the edges, tan in the center. Her hair was long and black, but tan patches circled her eyes and peppered her muzzle.

She was relinquished to SDHS when her elderly owner was hospitalized and no longer able to care for her. At the same time, the dog that Sheba had been raised with all her life, her canine companion, had passed away.

Before dogs were made available for adoption, they stayed in traditional, cage-front kennels, and for a few days, Sheba lay in hers with her eyes half-closed. She rarely lifted her head or stood up on all fours. She drank minimally and refused food. She was visited frequently by veterinarians, behavior trainers, kennel staff, and volunteers, but no one was able to get her to eat or go for a walk.

Then a goofy eleven-year-old German shepherd named Ranger arrived. Animal control officers picked him up off the streets as a stray, but his bright brown eyes flickered with such contentment that one would think he'd never been lost in his life. People marveled at his energy and enthusiasm. If a dog could two-step, I imagined Ranger would all day long. On walks, he twirled and pumped his legs in the air, his tail wagging in ecstasy over the new smells, sights, and people. His coat darkened from a sandpaper shade in the front to light brown in the back.

One day, a volunteer happened to walk Ranger by Sheba's kennel. She opened her eyes and lifted her head, scenting him. The volunteer brought Ranger closer, and Sheba stood up on all fours. She moved to the front bars, where the two dogs gently touched noses.

Sheba went for her first walk that day with Ranger by her side and ate her first meal with him in the kennel, too. Perhaps Ranger reminded her of the dog that had been in her life before or simply provided her with a sense of comfort that no one else could. Whatever the case, the two became inseparable. Sheba ate if Ranger ate. Sheba walked if Ranger walked. Sheba slept if Ranger slept. It became clear that if Sheba was going to survive, the two of them needed to be adopted out together. And in the end, they were.

Sheba and Ranger are now enjoying their golden years with two dedicated owners who cherish them, and with a beautiful backyard to play and sunbathe in. If Sheba could talk, I think she'd say that she was grateful for the day she stood up in her kennel and gave life another try.

Sheba probably didn't know she had done so the day she lifted her head to scent Ranger, nor how hard it would be to adapt to her new life. While Ranger had given Sheba the will to live again, she wasn't always comfortable in her new world. Her body was off the ground, but that didn't mean she knew how to move or where to go. That didn't mean she walked gracefully or with a lot of enthusiasm, especially under new circumstances.

In her new home, her owners told me Sheba was very anxious in the beginning, pacing and panting and whimpering at times. For the rest of her life, Sheba still had bouts of sadness, times when she wouldn't get up off the floor or eat.

But the important thing was that eventually she did.

She got up. She ate.

THOUGH I DIDN'T know it at the time, the morning Buster stood tall and I embraced him was the end of my relapse from hell. I finally found the courage to get up off the floor and ask for help, and as a result, life began to change. While I explored a new, more humble home inside myself, days and then weeks and then months of healthy eating passed. Danny slowly began to trust me again, and he stayed over at my place more and more.

Health was unfamiliar territory, however, and in the back of my mind, I was always waiting for the other shoe to drop. Or for me to just throw it down on the ground myself. Fear and anxiety were my constant companions. I sometimes didn't know what to do or where to go or how to move forward.

Everybody in my recovery group said that if I depended on my finite (not to mention crazy) mind and human power alone, it would only be a matter of time before I fell face-first back into food. For years they had said that there was a part of me beyond space and time, as pure and real as the eyes of a shelter dog, and I nodded and smiled. I said I would find a way to get in touch with that place, but secretly took it all as spiritual, touchy-feely bullshit.

I wasn't interested in addressing my mind or spirit, just the hands that wouldn't stop grabbing for more food, just the body that was never thin enough, just the physical part of this "disease." People, wise people, probably sensed this and warned me again and again that addiction was a deeper issue than I thought.

They said I would need to find my voice. To know what truly fed my spirit. To live in the moment. To be honest. They said that healing physically was only the beginning, but I didn't, or I wouldn't, hear them.

But I was beginning to hear them now.

The mere thought of relapsing made me want to die, so I figured I was in no position to refuse help from a friend, earthly or otherwise. My spirit was an ocean I'd been polluting for years, and the cleanup was far too big a job to do on my own.

So in the mornings, I found myself reading Eckhart Tolle, Pema Chodron, Hafiz, or Rumi. I bought a yoga mat and forced myself to sit on it for ten minutes with my legs crossed and palms up in the living room.

In the beginning, I found meditation to be about as comfortable as sleeping on ice. Nine out of the ten minutes, I closed my eyes and watched my mind give orders like a slave driver about what I needed to do that day, with occasional side comments about how terribly bad I was at meditation or life in general. One friend told me that the only rule to meditation was nonjudgment, and then I spent most of the time judging myself at how bad I was at not judging myself.

In an effort to make the experience less torturous and more compassionate, I tried "bowing to my heart" one morning, another suggestion from a friend. I got onto my knees and placed two hands over my heart, bowing over and over again on my yoga mat. I'm not quite sure how I got a bloody nose—I hadn't been hitting the mat with my face—but when I sat up and opened my eyes, I wiped my nose and a line of blood ran across my knuckles.

"Babe, I have a bloody nose!" I called to Danny in the bedroom. A few seconds later, he came out the door in his underwear with a box of tissues.

He laid me down on the couch and tilted my head back over a cushion. While he shoved tissues up my nostrils, he asked, "So how did this happen?"

"From bowing to my own heart," I said in a nasally voice.

"You must have bowed a little too hard," he said laughing.

Despite this, I continued to bow to my heart (injury-free) each morning and to practice various meditation techniques. Most of the time I felt like I had no clue what I was doing, but occasionally, I had brief glimpses of the fact that I was breathing, I was alive, I was here.

REGARDLESS OF MY fears and lack of confidence, a peace entered my heart again and again, and sometimes quite unexpectedly. I have to admit that the most serene time in my life so far wasn't in the presence of a dog or anywhere beautiful, but at a small Vietnamese restaurant.

Around six thirty on a Monday night, I sat alone at a table and slurped one spoonful after another of hot vegetarian pho. White steam and the sounds of vegetables sizzling in frying pans poured out of the kitchen double doors every time they swung open. The news blared on about a recent shooting, and a family in the booth next to me had a heated discussion in a language I didn't understand. I watched red brake lights flash in the parking lot outside the window as a fly buzzed around my table.

Suspended in the air, the fly beat her veiny wings a few inches from my face. I'm not sure if she was indecisive about where to land or just unable to stay in one spot for too long, but I could empathize with both scenarios. First, she landed on the edge of my water glass, then a knife on a peach-colored napkin, then the table ledge, and then on the outside of my wrist, where she paused to clean her delicate legs before flying away again.

I sat at the table for what must have been at least an hour, though I can't be sure because I completely lost track of time watching the fly and watching myself exist in such utter and inexplicable contentment. I couldn't keep myself from smiling as I chewed on soft tofu, carrots, celery, onions, and broccoli, and slurped up long, thin noodles from a bowl as big as my own head. Warm liquid traveled down my throat, the secret and silent part of me I'd abused for so long, and I don't know how to explain this, but every spoonful felt like forgiveness.

It occurred to me what a miracle it was that I'd gone from being unable to think about little more than food and my body to a life where calories and bingeing and puking never crossed my mind. To a life where my work was helping shelter dogs and making sure that I never climbed back into that dark hole of lies about who I was and what I deserved.

By the time I'd finished my soup, my lips hurt from happiness, my belly was warm and full, and my brain was calmer and quieter than it had ever been. To this day, I'm not sure why. But I learned that night that peace doesn't need a pretty place to live. It meets you wherever you are. Even in a bowl of pho.

When I left the restaurant, I remembered how dinner used to scare me as much as walking into a pitch-black cave. But I was not ashamed of that fact. Instead, I felt only more peace. More happiness. More tenderness.

At the simple thought of a black cave being filled with light, a warm bowl of soup, a girl with a belly full of noodles.

27

FOR THE NEXT two years, shelter dogs continued to rouse me out of bed and fuel me with passion and purpose each day. I often felt the steadiness of the earth beneath me. My body relaxed. My heart calmed. I went on walks and saw aspects in nature I'd never noticed before. I went to the recovery group with the desire to help not only myself but others. I cooked delicious meals for us from scratch. I moved back in with Danny and loved him better than I ever had. We even adopted our first dog together, a terrier-poodle puppy named Bella who, like Sheba and Ranger and Buster and every shelter dog I've encountered, assumed the role of my spiritual teacher from the very start.

One morning at six o'clock, a few months after the adoption, I decided that sitting up on my yoga mat was too much effort, so I got into child's pose, kneeling and lowering my head to the mat. I stretched my arms out in front of me while my meditation music om'd in the background, and my mind gave me a lecture about how lazy I was.

After two minutes, which felt more like two hours, a fluffy presence leapt over my arm. Danny usually kept Bella in the bedroom while I meditated, but I'd left the door open a crack, and she had nuzzled her way out, her paws so light on the floor that I didn't hear her coming.

When I opened my eyes and lifted my head from the mat, Bella stood a few inches from my nose, in between my out-stretched arms. In her mouth, she held a green frog toy by one leg.

"Bella, I'm meditating!" I said, but with a smile, because dear God was she cute! Five months old, four pounds, and not even a foot tall. Her coat of brownish black puppy fur was just starting to fade to creamy apricot.

Bella whipped her beloved frog so close to me that it hit my nose. Then, just in case I hadn't gotten the obvious memo that she wanted to play, she put her butt up, paws forward, and shook the frog between her teeth.

The meditation music changed to soft ocean sounds, and Bella blinked up at me with her chestnut eyes, pleading in all her adorableness for a game of tug-of-war.

I couldn't resist her. I grabbed a frog leg between my pointer finger and my thumb and gave it a little pull. Bella pulled back, letting out the most pathetic groan, which I think was meant to be a growl. Her tiny tail whipped back and forth, and I thought to myself, *I couldn't love you more if I tried.*

Our connection was wordless and relatively new, but I was already crazy about her. I loved every little thing she did. The time she leapt into a pond after a duck and kept going after him as though there was no difference between land and water. The way she assumed everything I had was hers, my glass of water, my food, my pillow, my socks, and never questioning whether she deserved it.

I loved how when I blew on her face, she gave the most pissed-off look and batted her dainty paw at my mouth. I loved how to everyone's shock, she thought "the cone of shame" was a fabulous accessory and wagged her tail when we slipped it over her head (this may be because I dressed her up on a regular basis). I loved how everything fascinated her, even dust.

I loved how after I gave Bella too much turkey and then Danny gave her too much salami, which caused an awful bout of pancreatitis, she didn't cuss out her mortified parents for feeding her too many treats. Instead, upon our return from a vet visit we couldn't really afford, she went straight to a warm patch of sunlight on the carpet. She didn't resent or complain. Right away, she got back to the business of basking in the warmth of the present moment.

I also loved how seriously she took the game of tug-of-war, as though she were some ferocious lion, and which Bella and I played that morning for almost ten minutes. I probably smiled the entire time, and when the timer on my phone went off to mark the end of the meditation, Bella's head tilted to the side. The sound startled me, too. We were still playing, and I'd completely forgotten that I was supposed to be meditating. Then again, if the point of meditation is to bring us to the present moment, maybe I was still doing what I was supposed to do.

While I leaned over to turn off the timer on my phone, Bella ran a few laps around the coffee table with her frog in her mouth. Then she came plummeting back toward me and spit him in my direction.

"Wow, what a performance for so early in the morning!" I said, clapping a little, and realizing that she was just the dose of lightheartedness that I needed.

Then, perhaps just to show me that there was more energy where that came from, Bella stood up on her hind legs, revealing her tiny pink belly with an orange X tattoo marking where she was spayed. She waved her two front paws in the air and I grabbed them with my hands. For a few precious seconds in the dim morning light, we danced.

I thought to myself, This is what meditation is about. Real joy. Real beauty. Dancing with my dog.

Then I scooped Bella up with one hand, and with the other, Daniel Ladinsky's translations of Hafiz, in *The Gift*. We moved to the couch, where Bella curled up on my chest, nose to tail. She smelled like oatmeal doggy shampoo, and her tummy growled for breakfast. I rested my head on her small back and felt her breathing calm. Then I flipped the book open to this poem and read:

Cast All Your Votes for Dancing

I know the voice of depression still calls to
you.

I know those habits that can ruin your life
still send their invitations.

But you are with the Friend now and look
so much stronger.

You can stay that way and even bloom!
Keep squeezing drops of the Sun

from your prayers and work and music and
from your companions' beautiful laughter.

Keep squeezing drops of the Sun from the
sacred hands and glance of your Beloved

and, my dear, from the most insignificant
movements of your own holy body.

*Learn to recognize the counterfeit coins
that may buy you just a moment of pleasure*

*but then drag you for days like a broken
man behind a farting camel.*

*You are with the Friend now. Learn what
actions of yours delight Him,*

*what actions of yours bring freedom and
love.*

*Whenever you say God's name, dear
pilgrim, my ears wish my head was missing*

*so they could finally kiss each other and
applaud all your nourishing wisdom!*

*O keep squeezing drops of the Sun from
your prayers and work and music*

*and from your companions' beautiful
laughter, and from the most insignificant*

*movements of your own holy body. Now,
sweet one, be wise.*

Cast all your votes for dancing!

28

FTER THE RELAPSE from hell, I decided to never set foot in a gym again, but crazy dance studios were just fine. I happened to find one I loved where a DJ in a purple Lakers hat played music in a corner booth during every class. A disco ball spun over the dance floor and life-size paintings of Justin Timberlake, Lenny Kravitz, and Britney Spears decorated the walls. Flat-screen TVs rotated ads for overpriced workout gear with quotes like, "Never never never give up!" and "Action creates!"

I took mostly hip-hop classes with an instructor I'd later see dancing beside Justin Timberlake on MTV, but one day I decided to give Zumba a shot. The instructor was named Sophia and completely insane. She had greasy hair, olive skin, and a six-pack. She made sounds that only a wild jungle animal could make and shook her hips so fast that I was just waiting for them to fly off. I had unwisely placed myself in the front row, and Sophia's sweat flung off her body and landed right on my face.

I shared the front row with a group of college students in Lululemon gear and bright blue sneakers, while the back row was made up of only two people: a teenage girl with acne and a nose ring, and one very fit woman who looked in her sixties and reminded me of Grandma Elsie because she hit every move on every beat, as good as any twenty-year-old. For twenty minutes we shimmied, quick-clapped, and hooted like monkeys.

I saw myself in the mirror, a broken piece of wood compared to Sophia's graceful curves. At one point I almost called it quits and faked like I needed a drink of water, but I took a deep breath instead. I closed my eyes, let the music pulse through me, and kindly asked the lips inside of my brain to stay closed. I didn't want to hear a word about self-consciousness between my ears.

Then Sophia demonstrated this move where she growled like a lion, squatted down, hit the floor, and bounced back up. We were to do this repeatedly, turning to face all four walls. The volume and speed of the music was turned up, and the lights around the room became pulsing orbs of color. I stopped and hunched over myself with a racing heart, wheezing and gulping air.

The grandma in the back row was not interested in the floor-smacking move, either. She had white curly hair pulled back in a scrunchie, a simple red tee, and navy blue workout shorts. There was also something gentle and joyous about her, something you couldn't help but notice in a room full of young women pushing themselves to keep up with Sophia, me being one of them. This older woman didn't seem interested in keeping up. Instead, to the beat of Shakira, she lifted her arms to the ceiling and swayed her hips. She closed her eyes and smiled as if visiting some beautiful place inside herself. The college girls and the teenager smacked the floor with looks of pain on their faces, while the old woman swerved her hands and fingers high in the air like a belly dancer.

I took her lead and did my own dance, too, feeling a little silly at first, but then thrilled. I shook my hair and head to the music. I crisscross-jumped and then spun around, just for the heck of it. I flicked my wrists. I kicked my legs. I bounced my boobs. I shook my ass. I did not let words like *flabby* or *weird* or *are people looking at me?* enter my dance party.

And after a few seconds of doing my own dance, I felt the strangest sensation that my body itself was a song. My arms and legs and head composed notes I'd never heard before, a perfect last-call song for the bars. My body was suddenly something to swing and sway to, something to relish like the best night of my life.

Something to celebrate.

29

IN 2011, DANNY sold his security business to a larger company, and after the acquisition, they recruited him to manage a division in downtown Los Angeles. With the sale of Danny's business, we could afford to move into a nicer apartment, and we fell in love with one just twenty minutes away from an animal shelter.

The shelter looked a hundred years old, but our apartment building was so new it reminded me of something you might see on *The Jetsons*. Everything had a silver tone to it: the tall, environmentally friendly buildings, the courtyards, the concrete, the resort-like saltwater pool. Mounds of fake grass and jacarandas separated one modern building from another, some of which contained a fitness club, conference rooms, and game rooms.

The move seemed a no-brainer, and within a month, we packed our things and changed zip codes, moving three hours north of San Diego. I was healthier, happier, and more confident than I'd ever been. While I was scared to leave the San Diego Humane Society, I knew that I would find a way to continue to work with animals. I'd heard about shelters in Los Angeles where the conditions were terrible and the staff desperately needed volunteer help.

So as soon as our boxes were unpacked, on a dreary morning, I visited the shelter around the corner. I parked in an almost empty gravel lot and stepped out of my car into the damp air. Even over the nonstop traffic in Los Angeles (people freak out when it rains and even nonbusy streets back up), I could hear a chorus of throaty dogs barking and crying.

Through an old red iron gate and past a bronze statue of a German shepherd leaping after a ball—all four legs extended, tail and ears high, tongue out—I followed signs toward the "Adoption Kennels." The shelter was almost deserted of people, probably due to the rain. I saw no volunteers or prospective adopters, just a kid a foot shorter than me with a yellow poncho on and two leather leashes draped around his shoulders. He nodded at me while cleaning his hands under a sanitizer dispenser. I nodded back and put the hood of my sweatshirt over my head.

Then I turned a corner and stared down an aisle of outdoor kennels cast in concrete and frighteningly reinforced with steel bars like a prison for incorrigible criminals. Wooden beams set a few inches apart were placed on top of the kennels to give the dogs some shade from the normally scorching sun, but they did little to shelter the dogs from the rain. It was sprinkling now, but that sky had poured an hour ago.

I desperately looked for any bedding, towels, toys, or bones inside the kennels—anything to comfort the dogs, warm the dogs, or to help relieve them of their stress. But there was nothing. Later, I'd find out that I was not even allowed to give the dogs a slim piece of rawhide, as just about anything clogged up the old drainage system.

In the first kennel, a fawn-colored pit bull with a patch of white on the chest jumped up on her hind legs and groaned, then barked. She shoved her wide muzzle in between the rusty bars, which were jagged after having been chewed on by so many restless dogs over time. She panted and stared directly into my eyes. A thick drop of water plopped on the top of her big head, and she pinched her tired eyes shut and shook her coat.

I knelt down on the concrete before her. After she sniffed my palm, she leaned all of her weight against the slick bars as though she wanted to melt into me. I blatantly ignored the signs that were everywhere (Please keep hands out of cages!) and reached both my arms around her shivering body, knowing from her demeanor, from her wagging tail and wiggly butt and loose stance, that she would not harm me. My hands moved from her flanks to her chest to the sides of her head, and she tilted it sideways while I stroked her behind the ears. They were cropped and her tail was docked close to her body.

I tried to keep 100 percent focused on her, not the screaming dogs all around me. Not the smell of urine and feces and unbathed dogs that was burning my eyes and throat. Not the yellow Lab down the aisle who was literally swimming on concrete, lying on her side and sticking both paws interchangeably through a small space at the bottom of the kennel in an effort to get out. Not the shih tzu mix a few kennels down with fur so matted it looked like dreadlocks. Not the wailing chow mix with a black tongue hanging out the side of her mouth.

When I dragged myself up off the concrete to continue walking down the aisle, a flash of pain shot through the nameless pit bull's eyes, and she shrieked loud enough for me to bend down again and stay with her for another few minutes.

"You're going to be okay, girl," I said over the deafening barking all around us, even though odds were that she wouldn't be.

ROW AFTER ROW, the dogs behaved as insanely as I might if I were trapped in a small space with nothing but my own feces, a water bowl, and some dried-up kibble. The majority of the dogs were pit bulls, but there were mutts of all kinds, and the smaller dogs were grouped together in twos or threes. I'd soon learn that small dogs were not allowed out of their kennels at all, a rule I never understood.

Some dogs licked the floors and paced nonstop. Some bit themselves until they bled and paced and chased their tails to no end. Many chewed on the metal bars of their door. And several looked physically ill.

I knelt down on the concrete and petted a husky with sky blue eyes, who licked my thumb, my wrist, and my forehead. I petted a Rhodesian ridgeback mix with a tall, muscular frame, a dignified face, and gleaming white teeth. I petted an old chocolate Lab mix with white hairs on his muzzle and bushy eyebrows, and a young shepherd mix who was jumping out of her skin to catch a pigeon scampering down the aisle. I petted some kind of poodle whose eyes I couldn't see behind her thick, matted fur, which felt like straw. And for long minutes, I stared at a heap of four white, wrinkly pit bull puppies who were trying to stay warm by cuddling in a pile. The one at the top of the pile twitched her legs in a dream, hopefully of some place beyond here.

Then I made my way toward the Cat Care Facility and the administration offices behind it, where, as hellish as I knew it would be on my heart, I signed up for the required training classes to be a volunteer. Perhaps I had managed not to cry while I explored the shelter because I knew I was there to sign up, and I didn't want anyone to think I couldn't handle it. But when I got into my car and looked back at the old building that contained so much suffering, and a rainbow spanned above it, an arc of color illuminated in the dim sky, I closed my eyes.

Then I cried.

30

WHEN YOU WALKED down the rows of kennels, eyes watched you from all directions. The dogs stared so intently, fixed on one solution, one vehicle for escape. I knew that intensity, believing that the harder you push yourself, the more you focus, the closer freedom will be.

All it took was one glance, one point of connection, to light most of the dogs up with hope. They believed that you might be coming for them. You might let them out. They barked and cried. They pulled you in. They stared you down, shoving muzzles between bars. They swiped their paws under the small space at the bottom of their kennel door as if to reach out and grab you to make your arrival happen faster.

I tried not to lead them on. I tried to look only at the dogs that volunteers were allowed to interact with. Some dogs picked up on the language of avoidance quickly. When you didn't acknowledge them, they understood that you were passing them by. You weren't coming for them. They broke eye contact and went back to chasing their tails or pacing at the bars or lying down with a heavy sigh.

But not Big Girl, a five-year-old, obese, red pit bull mix.

She was convinced that each person walking down the aisle was there to let her out, and she didn't have the patience to wait.

Big Girl often looked on the brink of a heart attack. The sun came down hard on her kennel, and even on the hottest of days, I never saw her anywhere but sitting at the front bars where there was no shade. When she wasn't barking and crying, she was drooling and panting. Her body heaved with short, dramatic breaths. Sometimes she lunged at the bars. They clattered and the noise echoed down the aisle, causing some of the dogs to cry and others to lunge at the bars themselves, as if the effect was contagious.

When I tried not to notice her, she only went more wild. Sometimes I thought she barked enough to explode. "Big Girl, calm down. Go back there where it's shady," I'd say, pointing to the back of her pen.

She'd look up at me as if I were insane, huffing hard, leaning the side of her body against the bars for petting.

ONE MORNING, I arrived at the shelter around eleven, an hour later than I usually did on weekdays. It smelled particularly awful that morning, with so many unbathed dogs and piles of poop drying out in the sun. I was a girl who enjoyed taking bubble baths and painting my nails, not to mention a typical person who preferred not to inhale gag-worthy fumes of shit, but nothing could keep me away from this place.

I volunteered a few times a week, and I regularly sat in pee, kissed pit bulls, and cleaned up poop and vomit. But it was worth it. Herding dogs, hunting dogs, bully-breed dogs, puppy dogs—I stroked them under the ears and on their bellies, kissed the tops of their dirty heads, held the weight of them, fed them, felt the shape and size of their tender paws. In return, the dogs took me as I was. And I'd go to that love any day, even if I felt like I needed a gas mask to do it.

Since I was late for my shift, most of the dogs I usually walked had already been out, so I made my way to Big Girl. I passed by another volunteer, who was a tall, older man wearing jeans and a Red Sox hat. He walked, or was attempting to walk, a young black pit bull. She wheezed and coughed and pulled on the end of the leash in all sorts of directions. He tried to control her, but she lunged toward me and jumped up, her paws landing on my thighs. He pulled her back and gave me a look that said, *Look what I've gotten myself into.*

I smiled at him and told him good luck.

"Who are you walking today?" he asked.

I pointed a few kennels down at Big Girl.

"No. I wish *you* good luck," he said.

MOMENTS LATER, I stood in front of Big Girl's kennel with a leash and took a deep breath. The bars shook as she threw herself against them. I hesitated and then I finally opened the door a few inches and slipped inside. Big Girl jumped on her hind legs, her paws landing on my shoulders. She grunted and pushed me up against the concrete wall. She bathed my face in slobber. "Okay. All right. Calm down, girl," I said. Every time I pushed her weight off me she jumped back up so that I was staring directly into her mouth, her pink tongue hanging out the side of it.

"Okay, Big Girl!" I yelled. "Sit!"

And then, magically, she did. She took a good three or four seconds to get into the sit position, slowly and consciously, as if concerned about doing it just right. In that moment, she reminded me less of a beast and more of a child, fragile and in need of praise.

"Good girl!" I said, stunned by her good behavior. I bent down and easily buckled the purple collar around her neck.

When the kennel door opened, she plunged out with me behind her. Her long, red tail whipped in circles. The dogs we passed screamed in their cages. Big Girl pulled while I water-skied the pavement behind her, leaning all of my weight backward to maintain some sort of appearance of control.

When we got out of the shelter, Big Girl dove toward a patch of grass. She squatted and peed for what felt like ten minutes. She tilted her head upward while noticing a crow on a telephone line. Her eyes squinted in the light. She scented the air, a concoction of trash from the sewer and car exhaust.

When she finished peeing, she began to walk leisurely, almost prancing by my side. There was no more pulling. I'm not sure if my arms or eyes were more shocked. No shelter dog I had ever walked before did anything but pull, as if they knew they only had a limited time outside their kennel and wanted to cover as much ground as possible. Someone in Big Girl's life must have potty-trained her and walked her on a leash before. Once, she had been someone's dog.

BUSY STREETS SURROUNDED all sides of the park. During our volunteer orientation, we had been warned about the traffic, warned not to let the dogs loose, told of accidents and dogs who had been hit. We were advised to follow a specific route in the park, which spanned about a block. The lush green grass hadn't been mowed in a while. There was a jungle gym and a stone fountain that the Humane Society had built more than a hundred years earlier as a resting place for horses. The fountain still sprayed fresh water, and the dogs I walked often dunked their heads into the basin to slurp it up.

Almost as soon as Big Girl and I stepped onto the park's grass, she spotted a squirrel and pulled hard. Her collar ripped apart. She made it halfway across the park in just a few seconds— picture Shaquille O'Neal winning a sprinting contest. I chased her at first, screaming in my mind, "Holy motherfucking shit! Fuck! *Nooo!*" Then I screamed out loud: "Big Girl, stop!"

She started running even faster, and while I huffed and ran a good twenty feet behind, it occurred to me that I could just let her go. I could let her run as hard and as fast as she wanted in the opposite direction of the shelter.

I thought of the sickening kennels. I thought about how minimal interaction with people and nature drove so many of the dogs insane. I thought of how unlikely it was for her to get adopted. And then I stopped running after Big Girl.

But in that very moment, she turned her head to look back at me while still running. Then she made a U-turn. Her body leaned so much to the left, I thought she might fall down. She came charging back in my direction and I wasn't sure if it was toward me or something beyond me. I wished her to stop. But here she came. Sprinting past two homeless women and their shopping carts. Past tall palm trees hailing her with their green hands.

Clouds of dust rose up behind her galloping paws. She looked weightless and powerful and like nothing that could be harnessed. When she was just a few feet away, I saw her legs kick back, almost bucking in the air.

Even though I was afraid, I squatted to her level and held my arms open wide. I caught her like a tidal wave. She knocked me backward and I bear-hugged her, wrapping my arms around her heavy body on top of mine. She slobbered all over my face. To the right of me, ants gorged on a Popsicle in the grass. To the left, somebody's sweatshirt hung off the monkey bars of an abandoned jungle gym. After about thirty seconds of holding her, I got up and lured her to the shade of a palm tree with some treats, the leash loosely wrapped around her neck, both of us panting.

There was no way I was going to try to get Big Girl back to the shelter without a collar. Most dogs resisted leaving the park and started to pull in the opposite direction about a block from the shelter. If Big Girl did that, she'd be running free down the road and risk being hit by a car, something that happened too frequently around these parts. My only option was to wait for a volunteer to come by.

Big Girl sat by my side watching every dead leaf or plastic bag that blew in the wind, every person in the distance, cocking her head at the sounds of horns and birds. The sun blazed in a cloudless sky. The grass looked like it was sitting on top of a giant mirror instead of soil, glimmers of light pocketing through the blades. The air somehow smelled like roses and fried food and smoke all at once.

I sat next to her and stroked her back, thinking about how easy it would be for Big Girl to run away. I worried that she'd see another squirrel, but then one passed, and then another, and she leaned toward them with interest but didn't try to chase. We sat side by side, eye-level, and sometimes she turned her head to look at me, I could see the black lines on the roof of her mouth, and how her teeth faded from white to yellow toward the back. Minutes passed. She was panting only a little now.

Big Girl put her head in my lap.

"See, girl," I said, scratching her under the ears. "This is what you need to do in your kennel. Just chill. Then people will know the real you."

But I knew what it was like to believe in something that didn't work, to mistakenly believe that if you did something long enough, the thing you needed would finally come.

TWO DAYS LATER, I waited in the shelter's front office, a small cluttered room with a donation bin for pet food, and I reeled under a growing sense of panic. I needed to know where Big Girl was. The pen where I'd seen her last now held two small dogs: an unneutered shepherd puppy and an elderly terrier mix whom he wouldn't stop humping.

There was a couple in front of me at the desk asking about their lost cat. The girl squeezed her boyfriend's arm, tears welling up in her eyes. Behind a pale blue counter, a young girl with a nose ring and shiny black hair typed the cat's information into an old monitor. She looked tired, unsympathetic, and young enough to still be in high school.

I leaned against an old sign on the wall that said, "If you care for them, help us care for them."

Behind the desk, a few dogs in the veterinary suite whimpered nonstop. An elderly woman sat on a bench sniffling with her head down, perhaps because she had lost an animal. A young vet tech in brown scrubs walked by holding three kittens in her hands. Every cell of my body said that Big Girl was gone. I just wanted everybody to stop moving and tell me where the dog I promised I'd take for another walk was.

Finally, the young couple turned away from the counter

holding a piece of paper listing other shelters where their cat might be, some highlighted. I stepped up to the counter.

"Hi, in kennel seventy-four, there is this young dog who won't stop humping the older one," I said. "I don't know if they should be kenneled together."

Without looking up from her computer screen, the girl said, "Okay, seventy-four, got it. Thanks."

"And there was this red pit bull that had been in that kennel for a month. Was she moved?" I asked.

"Do you know her ID number?"

"No. I called her Big Girl, but I don't know if other people did."

"I can't help you if you don't know her ID number," she said. "But I'll see what we can do about those two small dogs."

I nodded and thanked her.

"Oh wait," she said. "You mean K219834?"

"I don't know?" Most dogs didn't have names here. I never worried about their numbers, and called them what felt right.

She squinted to read the computer screen: "Five-year-old, red pit bull in kennel seventy-four?"

"Yes, was she adopted?" I asked, my heart beating in my throat.

The girl took a deep breath and shook her head. "No, she was not adopted."

I set both hands on the counter to hold myself up while an adoption counselor named Linda walked out of the veterinary suite. "Hey, Shannon," she said smiling.

This wasn't her fault. I knew that. But I pinched my lips together and turned around without acknowledging her. The front door of the office slammed behind me after I stormed out and ran down the concrete corridor, a tack board filled with pictures of stray dogs to my right, real stray dogs shoving noses between bars to my left. I burst through the front gates of the shelter and they slammed, too.

Big Girl could have changed a person's life.

I should have just let her run.

BEYOND ENRAGED, I paced down the sidewalk to my car. My body was a container that couldn't hold the anger. The sky had a hazy yellow glow, and I took the long way to where I'd parked, avoiding the place where Big Girl broke free from her collar forty-eight hours earlier. Still, I thought about it, I couldn't not think about it, how after a half hour sitting together under that tree, a volunteer never came.

I was the one who lured her back to the shelter, tossing one treat after another onto the sidewalk. Big Girl stopped to sniff the roots of old trees breaking through the ground, a random sneaker on the sidewalk, and gum, but for the most part, she kept her attention on me and the food. We had passed an organic grocery store, a row of outdoor cafes, and a five-foot banner on the side of the shelter promoting its behavior training classes.

And then we stood in front of a tall wrought-iron gate that looked like it had been built a century ago, back when the Humane Society not only took in abandoned animals but also abandoned children. You could hear the shelter dogs barking and crying behind it. Big Girl's body froze. Every muscle clenched. Her ears went back. I gave the collar a tug but she wouldn't move. The resistance seemed so intentional, so conscious. A bus promoting *Glee*'s new season whipped by then squeaked its brakes at a red light, but Big Girl didn't turn her head at the noise. With a frightening intensity, she stared at the front gate. Then she stared at me, or through me.

I began to plead with her. "Listen, I don't want to take you in there, but it's going to be okay. You're going to be okay. I'll walk you tomorrow. I promise."

The wind picked up and blew a few dead leaves and a Doritos bag. Big Girl started to pull in the other direction.

Out of fear that I'd lose her, I faked excitement. I dumped almost all of my treats on the ground. While she gobbled them up, I tightened the leash around her neck. When she finished the food, I called her name in a high-pitched voice, nearly shouting. I slapped my legs and jumped in the air. Her red tail wagged back and forth behind her while she watched. Each time I called her name, it seemed to light a spark in her. Maybe it was simply the sound of my voice, or the joy in being called something constant, or the idea that she might get more love and more treats. Maybe she took it as a clear sign that the walk wasn't over, but she responded to the energy as I'd hoped, following the pretend joy, the pretend possibility.

Then she did something terrible. She play-bowed and barked a distinctively different bark from that ceaseless, throaty roaring she did in her kennel. I'd never heard this sound from her before. It was playful, falsetto, puppylike, something you'd expect from a rowdy miniature poodle. I thought, *This was how she'd sound with a family, in a home.*

I opened the shelter gate and Big Girl trotted in behind me, as if we were just crossing through on our way to another park. Then the gate clanked shut and we stared down a row of cages. Everything about Big Girl stopped, her wagging tail, her panting tongue, her moving legs. She stared directly into my eyes with a look that said, *I knew I couldn't trust you.*

NOW, AS I unlocked the door to my car, that look, that horrible look, wouldn't leave me. I ripped off my volunteer vest, and a few Milk-Bone crumbs fell out of the pockets. I started the car and blasted the AC. The radio played Adele and I turned down the volume. I imagined Big Girl being taken out of her kennel to be euthanized. She must have thought she was going to the park again, but instead of going right, she went left. She was taken into a dark room and placed on a metal table instead of the cool grass. She was restrained instead of given the cherished chance to move her legs.

Did someone at least stroke her fur? Did she tremble? Did she get the feeling that any of this was her fault? Did she make a sound? Did she look at them in the way she had looked at me?

One needle to put her to sleep. One needle to stop her heart. And then she was gone. Quietly gone.

SOMEONE WAS WAITING for my parking spot and in typical L.A. fashion, honked at me because I was taking too long. I pulled out into the traffic and headed toward our apartment in a neighborhood once notorious for drug deals and prostitution, now a haven for high-end shops and Real Housewives. I passed a fit woman in a pink sports bra with an iPod banded to her arm. She ran with a purebred Lab by her side. I glared behind them at million-dollar condos—some concoction of hatred and envy consuming me. Did anybody living there know that within a mile, dogs were dying? Did anybody care about the number of lives being abandoned?

But then again, I had abandoned my father. He wrote to me every few weeks from jail after he got behind the wheel drunk and crashed into another family (thankfully, everyone survived). His sentence was for a minimum of a year, and he pleaded that receiving a letter from me would lift his spirits.

Writing the words "I love you" or "I forgive you" was easy. But bringing myself to send those words was much harder—I hadn't been able to bring myself to do it yet.

How far the mind can travel in seconds. First the idea that I was a bad volunteer, that I had let Big Girl down. Now I was a bad daughter, letting my father down. Shame, as it always does, hijacked my whole being and I could barely see the road in front of me, let alone past the irrationality of my own thinking. A feeling of dread surged through my bloodstream. Something about how I was a fake. Something about how I'd inevitably ruin everything, like I always did. Techniques I learned to manage my anxiety in therapy, "play the tape forward," "slow down," "breathe," were of no use to me now. I felt nothing but hatred and hunger. The two were still companions inside me, walking hand in hand, whispering that food would make it better. I hadn't seen these guys around in a while, but I couldn't fail to notice them now.

I made a quick turn onto the highway. I needed to find the people who would understand.

TWENTY MINUTES LATER, after a strangely almost traffic-free drive to West Hollywood, I pulled into a parking lot behind a church a few blocks from the Kodak Theatre. The church was tucked away in a suburban neighborhood, but signs of Hollywood were there—flyers for acting classes taped to mailboxes, a billboard promoting *Grimm,* houses piled onto each other, giving the area this claustrophobic feeling I still hadn't gotten used to in Los Angeles.

People of various shapes and sizes filtered through the doors of the ranchlike building behind the church: a few college students; a sexy woman at least six feet tall, who I'd later realize

was on a billboard for a tanning salon near my apartment; a
stylish gay couple holding hands; and a thin woman in her
twenties who wore a gaudy necklace that made her collarbones
into knives.

Five minutes passed. Then ten. I turned the radio on. Then
off. I almost left. Then decided not to. I had gone to recovery meetings back in San Diego all the time. Why had I been
avoiding them in Los Angeles? What was I so afraid of?

I remembered what Danny said to me a week earlier: "You
should be having the time of your life." And I had nodded,
because theoretically, he was right. I knew how lucky I was
to have the opportunity not to work, to wake up and do what
I wanted with my day. Never had I had such freedom before.
And yet here I was, not only not having the time of my life
but feeling myself move closer each day to some unnameable
darkness.

Perhaps the darkness was emotional burnout or compassion
fatigue from working at the shelter. Perhaps it was getting Dad's
letters and my paralysis about how to respond. Perhaps it was
that I hadn't realized how much I'd depended on my support
network in San Diego until I left it, how the routine of going
to work at the San Diego Humane Society and the familiarity
of life there had kept me afloat.

The clock blinked 12:05 P.M., five minutes after the meeting had started. Finally, I got the nerve to get out of the car. I
walked into a dimly lit room and took the only seat available,
next to a gorgeous man who wore a close-fitting white shirt.
He was tan, with broad shoulders and wavy blond hair. God, he
seemed too handsome, too beautiful to have anything to be sad
about. I smiled at him awkwardly.

Though everyone here seemed more eccentric and stylish than in San Diego, the meeting still had that same

we-are-in-this-together energy, and it made me breathe a little easier, though something inside me was still clenched tight.

An extremely tan and wrinkly anorexic woman handed out meditations for the group to read. A blackbird flew by a window in the corner of the room, then another, then another. Someone announced a three-minute meditation and pressed play on an old CD player. The sounds of waves and seagulls filled the room, plus a few coughs, heavy breathing, and the hum of an electric fan.

I had gotten off track from my daily meditation practice, and it felt almost impossible to sit still now. I wanted to be anywhere but in that chair listening to seagulls. Sometimes, peace is a dog that won't come when called.

Still, I closed my eyes. I counted my breath in and out a few times. Then the image of a blackbird came to mind. When, I wondered, was the last time I saw a bird struggle or pant when it flew? When did I see anything struggle when it did what it was born to do?

In the park, I had gotten a glimpse at what Big Girl was made for. She was natural, calm, and content in the great outdoors. She was a great companion. She was a different dog from the one who banged and lunged in her cage, the wild dog whom I mistakenly thought her to be.

Perhaps this was why the loss of Big Girl affected me so much: I had gotten her all wrong. She was a good soul, and I gave up on her before ever truly knowing who she was. The reason I hadn't interacted with her for the past month she was at the shelter was that I thought she wouldn't make it—she was too crazy—and I didn't want to pour my love and hope into an animal I was going to lose.

The meditation ended and I felt on the verge of tears. People around the room started sharing for three minutes at a time. "I can't do the things I want to do," a huge man with a beard and a deep, husky voice said. He was a recently divorced stand-up comedian wearing an orange Hawaiian shirt. Black curly chest hair poked out at the top. "I joke about my fat but you know what? I've tried to commit suicide twice. I pretend like it's funny, this weight, the fact that I can't fit on an airplane. I pretend like it's not a big deal."

Then a few other people shared, sounding whiny to me, sounding pathetic. Sometimes, when around so much honesty, I embraced it. But sometimes, I deflected; I hated it.

For most of the meeting, I chewed on my gum and tuned people out and looked through the window until an average-size woman in her thirties raised her hand. With blue hair, pink fingernails, and perfectly plucked eyebrows, she gave off a rock star/musician kind of vibe. She pulled at an elastic band wrapped around her wrist and said that when she tried to get on without her eating disorder, she felt like she was free-falling.

"I won't admit this to anyone but you guys," she said. "But food is not my problem. It's my solution. My God. My everything. You take my eating disorder away from me, and I don't know how to cope. I don't know who I am. I can't stand that feeling."

I remembered the one time I bungee jumped . . . how it felt like the sky was holding me by a string wrapped around my feet. The great distance between my head and the ground scared me, but when I screamed, it was more out of exhilaration than fear. If only I could learn how to dangle like that more in life, how to experience fear but not let it consume me.

My hand raised. "I moved here from San Diego a little bit ago," I said. "And this dog I really liked at the shelter where I volunteer, she's gone now. She's dead."

My gaze fell on an older man who was balding and

normal-size. He was nodding. The girl next to him with the boob job and fake eyelashes nodded, too. I had hated her ten minutes ago for sharing about how much she hated her size-zero body—and I wasn't oozing with love for her now, but I felt like she understood me.

"I don't believe in heaven," I continued. "But I can't believe that her spirit is gone. I guess I just want to know that wherever she is, she's okay. And I really don't want to eat over the not knowing."

My eyes moved from one person to another around the room, every head nodding.

32

THE NEXT DAY, I woke up around 7 A.M., two hours after Danny left for work to beat the traffic. I lay in bed and stared at the high ceilings, listening to the hum of a fan. A garbage truck beeped while it backed up outside the window and a familiar fog of depression settled over me.

Bella shook her coat and scratched at the sliding glass door. This was the signal that she wanted to use her porch potty. I cracked my ankles and got out of bed to open the door.

On our patio, the air was refreshingly cool, the sun bright. Above us, birds gathered on rooftops to call out their morning song, and thin, papery clouds stretched across a blue sky. "Peace is as close as my breath, peace is within me, peace is possible," I said silently, a mantra I'd begun saying back in San Diego. Bella peed and came back inside.

I got back into bed to sleep a few more hours, but just as my head hit the pillow and I pulled the covers over my face, I heard a muffling sound. Then Bella came sprinting out of the bathroom, bloody tampon from the trash in tow. She leapt up onto the bed and landed on my stomach with a thud, her tail wagging wildly, tampon between her teeth.

"Bella, no!" I sat up and yelled, which thrilled her. She

play-bowed and ran to the front door, where she lay with the tampon between her paws, gnawing on it like a bone. I took a step closer to her and she growled a little, guarding the stick that even I didn't want to touch, but which she found delicious.

"Fine," I said, and grabbed her leash.

As expected, Bella immediately jumped straight up into the air like a popcorn kernel. She dropped the tampon and I tossed it. Then I opened the door and followed Bella prancing down our echoey red and gray hallway, the ceilings and walls having been made with recyclable materials. In the elevator to the first floor, Bella growled at the sensation of movement like she always did.

BELLA, NOW A six-pound apricot fluffball whose cuteness can't be overstated, pranced more than walked. She bounced around with this innocent, delicate aliveness and wild curiosity that people, all kinds of people, couldn't help but smile about.

We passed a family Italian restaurant, a nail salon, a steak house where Danny and I met Dr. Drew a week earlier, and a posh hotel where the receptionist kept dog treats in a silver bucket and always gave Bella two.

It's hard to stay stuck in yourself when you are walking a really cute animal who wants to greet every person who passes, whether they are homeless or famous. I felt my mood lift in just being outside with Bella, and then when she spotted her favorite patch of grass.

Grass was somewhat hard to come by in Los Angeles, and when Bella found a grassy space, she behaved like I used to when I took a shot of whiskey, back when I used to be fun around whiskey. Bella more or less lost her mind, and got what we called "the zoomies," running in circles so fast that sometimes she fell over herself. To see her so thrilled about something as simple as grass made me laugh even on heavy mornings, as this morning was turning out to be.

After Bella was thoroughly "zoomed out," we walked to a trendy coffee shop, down the street near Urban Outfitters and Lululemon. There the barista asked me if she was a service animal. I pulled out my card to show him that she indeed was, and maybe because he was a teenager, he asked, "Well, like what service does she do?"

"She helps me," I said vaguely.

"With what?" he asked.

"Just . . . life," I said.

Bella had a few issues that made her "emotional support animal" status questionable, like a bad habit of pooping in bookstores and barking incessantly at security guards. As a puppy, she barked at everything that moved, including wind. But for the most part over the past two years, she was the small presence I found myself reaching to hold, and talking to, more often than anyone else. Before moving to Los Angeles, Bella came to work with me at the Humane Society every day. She slept on my lap or under my desk, and I could hold her or pet her instead of visiting the nearby vending machine for some stress relief.

"I think I need to get me one of those," the kid said.

"It would probably be good for all of us to have one," I said.

Both of us stared down at my utterly content dog, tail slapping against the wood floor, ears perked, eyes lit up at the simple sound of her name.

I SAT DOWN with my coffee at a small table by a window with Bella in my lap. U2 played faintly in the background. A beautiful woman in a business suit walked in wearing a blinding diamond that demanded attention. Two cyclists whipped by the window. The cash register binged as it opened and closed, and I pulled out a letter from my father that had been in my purse for days.

Every time I got a letter from him, I was afraid to open it, as if reading his sober words would throw the pain of hoping for a father again back into my heart. After a few years of trying to distance myself from his alcoholism, I'd deluded myself into thinking that because I had cut off contact, I'd freed myself from the pain, as if emotions were gears I could choose to shift in and out of, as if I could turn the reality of his disintegrating life off by simply refusing to see it.

So I tried never to think about Dad. I stopped watching UConn games. I didn't listen to the Counting Crows or the Beatles anymore, even though I loved them both. But no matter what I did, my love for him lived on. Every Father's Day and every phone call from him hurt, and I was afraid of that hurt, afraid my heart-sadness might devour me in the way I used to devour cookies.

When my friends started having babies, I was jealous of their family lives. When I saw a picture of a young dad putting his two-year-old daughter up on his shoulders, I felt the urge to warn the little girl not to love him so hard, not to believe he was her hero, because then if he crumbled, she would crumble. She'd reach the age when she was supposed to be an adult and she would be far from it, having gotten up on the shoulders of so many other things, some of which almost killed her. She'd find herself at eighteen or twenty-five or thirty, pretending she was much stronger than she felt, pretending she didn't still ache for the light in her dad's eyes to come back.

I looked down at the envelope address and inmate number.

Near the number, Dad's cell mate, who was an artist, drew a picture of a dog that looked strikingly like Bella, a cream-colored little mutt with black beady eyes, tiny, floppy ears, and a feather-duster tail.

I opened the two-page letter. Dad said that he was sorry for the things he'd done. He wished it hadn't come to this, but he was trying to make the best of it. He was reading a lot, gardening, and most important, sober for good. He was leading meetings, and he was doing "great."

In jail, my father struggled with the same thing I did in Los Angeles, which was to acknowledge the truth. To say, *everything isn't perfect. I'm still having a hard time. I'm afraid if I start to feel, my pain will overtake me.*

Through the overly peppy tone of the letter and the perfectly clean cursive handwriting, all I could feel was his shame. He believed that he was the things he'd done, that there was no difference between him and his alcoholism, the man and the disease. He believed he had to convince me, and the world, of his goodness.

And I knew this feeling. It was enough of a reason, I thought, for anyone to drink for the rest of their life.

33

WHEN YOU'RE ON the euthanasia list, you don't know it.

You know you are suffering. You know this is not the place you want to be. Maybe, if you are smart, you sense that your life is in danger, darkness is coming, but you don't believe you are going to die.

When the same person who feeds you takes you outside your cage and walks you past lots of cages just like yours, you think, *This can't be a bad thing. This might actually be a good thing.* Maybe you're walking toward freedom. Toward comfort. Toward light.

But then you're in a cold room with either too much light or no light at all. The people there, their energy feels funny.

And even when you see the needle, you don't know what it means.

Even on your last breath, you don't know where it goes. Where you will go.

FIVE MONTHS AFTER arriving in Los Angeles, and at a club just a few blocks from my new apartment, I threw my head back to take a shot at the bar, something I hadn't done in years.

Tequila trampled down the tracks of my throat and burned in my chest. I set the glass down and sucked out the last juices of a lime and closed my eyes tight and opened them.

A long mirror hung across the back of the bar and I tried not to look at my reflection. I'd spent the day at the shelter and looked like it, too. My cheeks were sunburnt, eyes tired, hair in a wet, messy bun since I didn't have time or desire to dry it.

Beautiful women with thin and busty bodies were all around me in short dresses and high heels. The comparison started automatically. This one was prettier than me. But I was prettier than that one. She was fatter than me. But I was thinner than that one. The best-looking person in the room also became the safest, the happiest, the one with a perfect life. Once again, my brain kicked out a song that hadn't played in a while: "Thin plus pretty equals happy." I still knew all the lyrics. My head started to nod. I almost got up to dance. Secretly, a voice said yes.

I ordered a beer for Danny, and a water for Julie, who had recently moved from Connecticut to a studio apartment down the street from us. Kanye West's new song came on the speakers and a few girls screamed. It was midnight and there were enough drunk people around to crowd the dance floor. Danny and Julie were somewhere behind that dance floor sitting at a small table near the DJ booth. We were celebrating the fact that after seven years and three thousand miles between us, Julie had finally moved to the West Coast.

While waiting for the drinks, I leaned on the cool, silver bar and peeled off the Band-Aid on the back of my wrist. The cut was about an inch long, still raw and pink, but also damp from the antibacterial ooze Danny rubbed on it when I got home from the shelter.

Mama, a three-year-old red, Rhodesian–pit bull mix, hadn't meant to scratch me. She had meant to scratch the dumb, suicidal pigeon who flew into her kennel right after I slipped inside and clanked the door shut behind me.

Mama leapt onto her hind legs to swat at the bird, who flailed against the barbed wire at the top of the cage. I screamed and crossed my arms in front of my face to block Mama's lunges while the dogs all around us went wild. Feathers fell. Mama snapped her teeth in the air, snarled, and revealed her black gums. Shelter staff came running. They restrained Mama and freed the bird, while I tried to hide the gash on my arm so Mama wouldn't be put on "bite quarantine" and potentially move up higher on the euthanasia list.

The drinks came. I sealed the Band-Aid over my cut and squeezed through the crowd holding beer and water. The song changed to Rihanna. A champagne bottle with a sparkler lit from inside moved past me on a tray. Dim bodies reflected in the floor-to-ceiling mirrors. I moved through the smoke and fog, past girls and guys holding hands, glossy lips, a girl with a cherry-red leather jacket and a long white dress. Another girl with an obvious boob job and plunging neckline made me walk around her. There were clinking glasses and vinyl padded chairs. There was Julie, somewhere, dancing. This was pure Hollywood. Glamour. The allure of feeling important.

Danny wore a black polo and sat on a pleather white couch, typing into his BlackBerry and nodding his head to the beat.

"That took a while," he said. Under a pink strobe light, I noticed a part of his black hair that was thinning by his ears. I kissed his forehead and inhaled a strong whiff of his cologne. Then I stood at his side and scanned the crowd for my sister, my fingers on his arm.

Danny put his hand on my hand and kissed me. Then he pointed to the corner of the dance floor and said, "Your sister has been getting down."

Under a yellow spotlight, Julie danced in her own little circle, doing some sort of scooping motion with her hands. She reminded me of the first time I brought her to the shelter, how she reached both of her tiny arms up to her shoulders through the bars, her right cheek pressed against the metal to reach even farther, lifting small dogs into her hands and off the ground. Poodles, terriers, shih tzus, and Chihuahuas: "They don't want to be touched, they want to be held," Julie had said. Later, she told me there wasn't a worse feeling in the world than letting the dogs go, than putting them back down.

I came up to Julie and grabbed one of her hands and spun her beneath my fingers. The red highlights in her hair shimmered. When she blinked her eyes, I could see the gold eye shadow over her lids, purple in the creases. She wore hot pink heels, a black dress, and a locket I'd given her. She smelled like the fruity perfume our mother had given us last Christmas. I dipped her in my arms and we danced like we did as kids, before we ever cared about trying to be sexy, before sex had anything to do with how we saw ourselves.

But at some point while we were dancing, I looked down at my stomach and then I couldn't stop looking down. My stomach was too round, too fat, too full. Shame and resistance erupted deep in my belly and traveled up my throat. My mind swelled. A voice said, "Why did you have four pieces of pizza for dinner?"

And then came the familiar doubling of myself. Part of me was on land, dancing with my sister, pushing sweat back into my hair, snapping pictures with my iPhone, laughing hard, keeping the guys who could never have Julie off her.

Then there was that other part of me stepping onto an old boat, untying the ropes that connected me to the dock. I was leaving, drifting, letting that strong wind take over and blow the focus off my sister and onto the pizza I had for dinner, a meal I'd had dozens of times in the past few years without any trouble.

"Get empty!" screamed the voice that only I could hear. I tried to ignore it, the fact that my insides were reorganizing, something both subtle and massive happening beneath my skin. I felt heat, nausea, a jittery sensation. The more I tried to turn my attention outward, the louder and deeper the voice seemed to get.

No, stay present.

"Get empty," the voice said again, without hesitation, as if it already knew I was in its grip.

I tried to reenter the state of playfulness that my sister and I were in just moments earlier. I spun Julie around but the urge persisted, this urge that had been gone, miraculously gone, for almost three years now.

"I'm gonna go pee," I heard myself say to my sister. Then I pointed to Danny. "He has a water for you if you need it."

"Good, I'm dying!" she yelled over the music. She headed to the couch where Danny was sitting, and looked back once, smiling.

I MOVED THROUGH the crowd to the bathroom, where women primped in front of a long gold-rimmed mirror above a black marble counter with three sinks. A Hispanic woman, perhaps in her fifties, sat on a bar stool at the end of the counter. Beside her was a tray filled with perfumes, mints, hairspray products, and neatly folded white towels. She smiled at each woman who barely noticed her, these women primping and chatting and sometimes slurring at their reflections in the mirror.

When it was finally my turn, I went into the middle stall.

I knew that I couldn't get all the pizza out of me since it had been hours since dinner, but at least I could get something. I could feel a little less full, a little less disgusting.

I pulled my jeans down and sat on the toilet. I figured I could throw up between my legs, quick and quiet like I used to back in the college dorms. The music was blaring, a Lil Wayne song now, and women were nearly shouting over each other outside my stall. No one would know. And this would just be one time. I'd get back on track tomorrow.

I put four fingers in my mouth. Girls outside the stall talked about a picture they'd taken:

"Do I look fat in this pic?" one said.

A heel stomped on the tile floor. "Jesus, you're a twig. You're a sexy mama and you know it," said another.

Mama.

It was the last thing I wanted to come into my mind right now, but there she was. My mama. Her blue eyes. How she visited me in rehab and used the bottom of her gray T-shirt like a tissue. "Don't you understand?" she cried. "We are all the beautiful things we say we aren't."

My fingers partially came out of my mouth so that my nails rested on my front teeth. Then I set my hand down on my thigh. I pulled some paper out of the dispenser, wiped the spit off my fingers and chin. I dropped the paper into the translucent bowl, pulled up my jeans, and walked out of the stall.

I went to the sink nearest the Hispanic woman to wash my hands at the counter, to make sure my eyes weren't red or bulgy. The faucet water was ice-cold then lukewarm. When I was about to dry my hands with a paper towel, the woman tapped my shoulder with one arm, her other arm outstretched, holding a clean white towel.

She motioned for me to give her my hands. I held them out. She took each hand, one at a time, and patted it dry. We both looked down at the towel, not at each other. And her attention to my hands, her thoroughness in drying them, made me feel profoundly guilty.

34

A T 10 A.M. the next day, the room spun and the shades let in too much light. I got out of bed and found Tylenol in our bathroom. I felt hot, nauseous, secretive, still in the grip of something. Danny was sleeping, snoring a little, enjoying a precious Saturday when he didn't have to be up at the crack of dawn for his job downtown.

I hadn't told him what happened in the bathroom last night. I knew he wouldn't judge me—Danny had seen me have an emotional breakdown about a potato chip before, and much worse—but I didn't want to acknowledge how close I had come. Not to him. Not even to myself.

I splashed some water on my face and swallowed the Tylenol. Part of me wanted to understand how I ended up with my hand in my mouth, why I drank like I was on spring break back in college . . . but more of me wanted to just pretend it never happened.

Bella jumped off the bed and shook her coat. Like most dogs living in the comfort of a home, she woke up thrilled every day. She stretched her front and back legs, then arched her head upward for a good stretch of the neck. She pawed at the bedroom door, which meant that she wanted me to open it. I did. She had me well trained.

In our small kitchen, I fixed Bella her food, which was disgusting but the only thing she would eat: raw duck. Sometimes she wouldn't even eat that. Sometimes she'd circle the plate ten times before taking a bite. Danny joked that maybe she needed to come to my recovery group.

I set Bella's food down near the sliding glass door that overlooked other apartments, then stood in the exact spot Bella required me to stand if she were to eat, three feet away.

Bella began circling the plate. Through the window, a white cat stood on the rails of the balcony across from our apartment. She was a purebred Persian with a pink collar and sea-green eyes that I could see from a distance.

I stared at the cat hard, as if my watching could help her. She was just walking on that thin railing as if she had all the room in the world. I could see the wind blowing her fluffy fur to the east, one missed step and she'd fall God knows how many feet.

But then she leapt off the rail and safely onto the stone balcony, prancing through the open glass door back into the apartment.

I exhaled.

Bella continued circling.

Then, finally, she took a bite.

A FEW HOURS later, my sister came over. The pool at my apartment complex smelled like Banana Boat sunscreen and peanut butter. Only two kids were there: a boy with a red bathing suit and matching goggles, maybe five years old, and a younger girl in a blue-dotted bathing suit with Dora the Explorer on the front.

They took turns leaping off the edge of the pool into the arms of a tall, balding man who appeared to be their father.

Julie and I sat on the steps watching behind our big sunglasses. We were both slightly sunburnt, with our long hair down and sticking to the back of our necks. Reggae music played in the background and Julie nodded her head to the beat.

She was excited to finally be on the West Coast, and hoping to get a salon job in Hollywood. While still petite, she'd grown into a beautiful, strong woman. She'd faced her own challenges over the years, and she overcame them with a level of raw-hearted courage I admired. She also seemed to have no problem writing and reconnecting with Dad now. A tattoo of linked chains ran down from Julie's elbow to her wrist, an infinity symbol, signifying her limitless love for Dad.

The kids in the pool seemed so utterly absorbed in their play, in their little waves. The father splashed his hands and made ripples in the water. Then he held the fingertips of the little girl while she floated on her belly and kicked her feet behind her. He moved his daughter from one side of the pool to the other, both of them gleaming in the sunshine. The son did handstands and somersaults on his own in the shallow end and yelled at his dad occasionally, "Look, Dad! Watch this!"

And the dad would watch with such a distinctive look of pride and love in his eyes.

I thought about how my father had once looked at me that way, too. If his eyes weren't so blurred and bloodshot now from not being able to put the bottle down, he still would. Love wasn't the thing that went missing inside him. He didn't lose his love. He lost his sanity.

Julie chugged some water, then yawned loud and stretched her arms wide. I thought about telling her what happened at the club, about how lost I'd been feeling lately. I thought about letting her know that when I closed my eyes to meditate, I saw the dogs I couldn't save and the dad I couldn't write and the puking girl I used to be and was afraid of becoming again. I knew I should relax, take it easy. I just couldn't seem to do it.

Julie, never one to resist a body of water for long, said, "Well, I've gotta get in there."

Then she cannonballed into the pool to ensure that I got wet. She did the breaststroke back and forth, rising above the water and taking a deep breath, then submerging herself underwater again. Sometimes she paused in the shallow end and stood with beads of water trickling down her cheeks. She scrunched her hair like a dish towel, blinked a few times in the light. From a distance, I could see water caught in her long eyelashes.

The dad swam his daughter right by me, "There you go, Dianne!" he said. "There you go!"

Julie was back in the deep end now. She floated on her back, arms and legs stretched, eyes closed, a look of calm across her face.

I wasn't going to bring up my issues and ruin this goodness. Not today.

35

THE NEXT DAY, I opened the door to the volunteer office, which was inside a trailer behind the dog kennels. A blast of AC hit me and strangely, the smell of mint. A PC that volunteers used to sign in with was one of the only signs of the twenty-first century in this small space. A few animal welfare ads from the early nineties covered the walls. There was a stack of animal behavior books, the bindings shredded and worn down, next to the computer. A handful of behavior trainers, who not only worked with the shelter dogs but offered classes to the public, also had their desks crammed into the trailer.

A girl my age was signing out. She looked exhausted and was covered in dog hair but at least she had sneakers on. The last time I saw her, she wore flip-flops in the kennels and I couldn't imagine the number of paws that stepped on her toes or the pee and poo that found its way in between them. She also had on dangly earrings then, which the first puppy she came across would surely find too tantalizing not to play with. Today, she had on no jewelry.

"Stay cool out there," she said on her way out the door. "It's already so hot."

I told her that I'd try, even though I knew it was impossible.

I signed in, put a fern-green apron on over my clothes, and pinned my name tag to the front of it. On the counter next to the computer were large Ziploc bags of dog biscuits. Baking treats was one way that people could volunteer their time to the shelter, and it was a popular job. I rarely saw the counter without a bag of cookies, and today, the treats were soft, warm, and oddly Christmas themed even though it was summer. I touched them and smiled at their freshness. I doubted this mattered to the dogs, but it made me feel slightly better. I hated giving them stale treats that the smaller ones struggled to bite into.

For the first hour, my attention went to three matted poodles, an old Chihuahua with an underbite, and a black pit bull who'd recently come into the shelter with red-painted toenails. And then, while I walked from one kennel to the next tossing Santa Claus cookies inside, I saw a black nose pushing out between the bars of the last kennel, in the very back corner of the shelter.

I walked up to that nose and before me stood a pit bull so skinny that even her shadow looked bony. Her tail, a little stump of a thing, looked like it had been chopped in half and then stomped on in three places. From her rigid shoulder blades to the bones jutting out of her hips, a wild, joyful energy moved through her. She wiggled and I cursed the bastard who had starved her. Her eyes were so intensely expressive and filled with brown, green, and gold hues. She looked as though she were on the verge of speech, of saying something sad but true.

I squatted and reached my arms through the bars. She leaned into me with eagerness. She twisted her head to look up into my eyes, squinting in the sunlight. My fingers sank into her rib cage, and I felt her breath on my face, a disgusting stench, yet I moved my face in closer. She had a blaze of white across her chest, and brindle fur that looked gray from a distance but up close was a combination of gold, blue, and red. A white paper above my head said that her name was Sunny, ten months old.

The heavy metal door creaked and clanked behind me as I slipped inside. I knelt down, avoiding eye contact so as not to intimidate her. Sunny came right to me, nestling her nose into my stomach.

I had long ago stopped caring about getting covered in dog poop or breaking out on my face from being kissed by dogs who had likely licked their own crotches minutes earlier. But there was a particularly nasty smell in Sunny's kennel that made even me gag, something like pee and sewer water, but you could have multiplied it by a hundred and I still wouldn't have left. I sat down with my back against the concrete, legs stretched across the length of the kennel. Sunny gladly sprawled across my lap.

I could touch her anywhere. Her toenails, the tough gray pads of her paws, her broken tail, her pointy hips, her tongue. She trusted me with a kind of faith that I felt I didn't deserve. I was just another small person watching too many dogs suffer. Wishing I could do more.

Like many pit bulls, her face reminded me of a frog. She had black whiskers and lighter fur around her muzzle than the rest of her head. Her ears, unlike her tail, hadn't been cut. They flopped over themselves and perked up whenever she heard a sudden noise.

Here we were, I thought, dogs screaming all around us, metal clanking, shit stinking, animals on lists to die without knowing it yet, and Sunny's eyes couldn't have been brighter than the pulsing rays of sunlight beaming down on us. I felt that my presence had something to do with those eyes, and it made me feel like I mattered. Thoughts about what happened at the club and life in general, those lovely, ever-frequent, subtle, negative thoughts, took a backseat to an intense connection in the moment with someone who wasn't human.

For a few minutes, I petted Sunny and let her lick my fingers. A handful of flies swarmed about her head and kept landing on her tongue as if it were a pink couch they were intent to lounge on. Then a fire truck drove by the shelter with its sirens blaring. Sunny raised her head and tilted it with interest. Several dogs around us started howling, but this sound was nothing like the plaintive barks and cries I heard all day, the voices of animals confused and scared. This howling was born from something elemental and profound, and it actually made me smile.

The mutt diagonally across the aisle from us held her mouth in the shape of an O, snout to the sky, eyes closed. She surrendered to that primal force within herself that said, "Howl," and howl she did.

It was the sound of resilience, the sound of a dog's primitive essence surviving in the barren kennels—I could have listened to that music all day long.

SOME OF US howl by writing a poem. Some of us howl by singing, or connecting with another on a deep level, or dancing, or praying. We do what confirms without words who we are, where we come from, what makes us unique.

A power from within can persist in the darkest of places, an incalculable force that has a contagious effect.

I'm not just talking about the will to survive, but the need to feel one's own aliveness. Even as we're dying. Even in captivity.

Sometimes, what upset me more than dogs being euthanized was when they stopped acting like dogs. They began pacing back and forth at the kennel bars like robots. They stopped cocking their curious heads at the fat pigeons strutting down the kennel aisles. They refused to lift their eyes from the concrete. They lost their desire for food or to even drink in the world through their nostrils, scenting as all dogs do. They stopped being the creatures they were meant to be.

Their ability to howl, or to know the place where the howl came from, was gone.

AFTER THE FIRE truck had passed, I picked up one of the many stale treats on the floor. Another volunteer must have tried feeding Sunny earlier, or tossed treats into the kennel. I placed the kibble in my flat palm and held it in front of her nose. She closed her eyes and looked away. Her tail, had it not been so broken, might have tucked.

"Hey, girl, you got to eat," I said.

She lowered her head into my lap and closed her eyes. The howling had stopped completely, and the normal, ear-piercing screaming and crying had started up again. I stroked Sunny's fur and counted the bones to her rib cage.

"Sunny," I said, my chest tightening. "I'm not doing everything I could be doing. I'm tired of going to meetings and worrying about taking steps backward and what will happen when Dad gets out of jail and if he is going to be okay and if I'm going to be okay."

I leaned over and hugged her. "Do you worry, girl?" I asked. "Do you remember your life before here?"

She lifted her head again at the sound of a question. Her neck tilted slightly. Her eyes were auburn, alive and glistening. She sniffed the air, then sniffed my neck, her wet nose on my skin.

36

THE NEXT TIME I went to the shelter, Sunny was waiting as usual with her nose through the bars. The same joyous greeting came bumbling toward me, followed by the same slobbery plopping into my lap. We sat together for five minutes, her nestling her body as close as possible to mine, me admiring that ever-expressive face.

We sat near a pipe that jutted out from the wall at the back of each kennel. Positioned just above a metal water bowl, the pipe would pour out water to fill the bowls each hour. The water then flowed over the bowls and washed down the kennel floors, slanting slightly toward a drain. Some of the pee and poo was washed away, but never all of it.

I can't tell you how many small dogs, poodles and Chihuahuas especially, performed a terrified dance with all four paws, lifting them up interchangeably every time the faucet turned on. With their tails tucked and eyes wide, they wailed at the sight of the rushing water, unable to stop it from going halfway up their little legs.

Just as I was thinking about the drainage system, wondering exactly how old it was and how much money it would cost to get a new one, the water turned on. I leapt to my feet and so did Sunny. Other dogs cried and barked, some screamed.

Sunny hid behind my legs like a child and whimpered a soft, breathy cry. The water rushed beneath our combined feet and paws. Sunny's ears went back while she pushed her head against the side of my knee. She leaned her body into mine so heavily, as if she wanted to disappear. Her skinny legs shook unsteadily as she stared intently at the faucet, whimpering until the exact moment it turned off.

"It's okay, girl, it's just water," I said.

She didn't seem convinced. For minutes after the faucet turned off, Sunny wouldn't turn her head away from the bowl. Picture a cat staring at a mouse hole. I waved my hand in front of her face to break her concentration. She didn't blink. She seemed horrified.

Then, she came out from behind my legs. Saliva dripped from her mouth. Her chest heaved. Her tongue was dry. I knew she was thirsty, excruciatingly thirsty in this heat. She took a few steps toward the bowl, a few steps back. A few steps forward, then back. Wet paw prints marked her dance between me and the bowl.

She yawned, a sign of stress, then stood over the bowl, filled to the rim with water. She looked down and I thought she might take a lick, but her eyes widened and she let out a whimper and backed away. I realized what she was afraid of: her reflection.

The bowl was stainless steel, and the water moved slightly inside it, vibrating from the sound of barking dogs all around us. Sunny's body told her to drink, but her mind told her a scary, dangerous dog was in her way. My mind lied to me, too. I took a few steps to the bowl, peering down myself.

The face looking back at me wasn't special. I wore no makeup or jewelry, and a clump of dirt had brushed against my forehead, leaving a dark smear. Yet how much happier I was with this picture than when I sometimes stood in front of a mirror all done up, examining my makeup and body with a fine-tooth comb.

"Pain is beauty," I'd said more than once. But maybe that phrase had less to do with wearing high heels and suffocating push-up bras and more to do with looking for validation and security in what is bound to change and ultimately fade away. How many moments of my life passed when I was consumed by my appearance, and how many still did, and what did that ever get me but pain?

I dipped my finger in the bowl, then held it in front of Sunny's mouth. Her eyes nearly bulged out of her head. She backed away to the opposite wall. Then she slowly approached the bowl again. She twisted her neck to turn back and look at me. Her ears unclenched, and her body loosened.

And then, as if she made a decision, like she was standing on a cliff and saying "fuck it," she jumped. She dunked her mouth inside the bowl and drank and drank in big gulps. I gasped and watched her stomach expand. She came back to me gloriously slobbering, looking like she felt a lot better, like this was the first nourishment she'd given her body in a long time. I nearly stood up screaming and cheering, nearly became liquid myself.

I knew this feeling. How loud a body can beg. And finally, the taste of water.

WE REPOSITIONED OURSELVES near the back of her kennel, where the shade cast a shadow of relief on us. I sat down with Sunny lying across my lap and pulled out a brush from my volunteer vest pocket. I grazed it along her back, the bones of her spine protruding. Sunny shivered at first, but unlike the last dog I tried brushing, she didn't think the brush was a chew toy.

I used it easily and she seemed to like the sensation, her face relaxing, her weight, slight as it was, slumping down.

Relaxation came over me, too. Sometimes, in an environment with so much anxiety and screaming, I felt safer than when I was alone with myself in a quiet room. My thoughts had less power here, less of an ability to corner me into this lurking sense of dread I'd had since I was a teenager: *plan all you want, but life can still implode.*

In the weeks since almost relapsing at the club, I'd started to get back into my daily meditation practice and going to more recovery meetings. But nothing helped me to deal with fear and anxiety like animals. More so than any other place, here in a dog kennel, my mind cleared. I could sit with Sunny and realize, *All this shit I'm terrified of, it's not here with me right now. But a dog who needs me is.*

Clumps of Sunny's fur hovered in the air around us and landed among the scattered biscuits on the floor, too many to count. The anorexic girls I met in rehab, the ones who lost clumps of hair due to malnourishment, came to mind. One girl, whose skeletal face made her eyes and mouth look like craters, swore that her appearance was not due to weight loss but an undetected form of cancer. She didn't see a severely underweight person in the mirror, like the doctors said she was, and I believed her. I knew body dysmorphia and how what isn't real can become a concrete fact in one's own mind. Becky was the girl's name. She often pulled strands of black hair off her baggy clothes during group therapy and joked that she was shedding.

I wondered where Becky was now. I petted Sunny, hair falling out between my fingers, and wondered if Sunny was shedding healthily, or if this was because she was starving, too.

"Sunny, you have to eat, okay, girl?" I said, setting the brush down and pulling out some treats from my pocket.

I broke up a soft treat and offered it to her in tiny pieces, making num-num sounds as if she were a baby, then pretended to eat the treat myself.

At first she looked at me bewildered. Then her tail stopped wagging. She buried her head into my stomach as if to say, "Please, stop." The other stale treats on the ground didn't encourage me to keep trying.

37

ON THE WEEKENDS, the shelter was at its busiest. But
since Sunny lived in the back corner, people walked
by only occasionally. Whenever someone did, I lowered my head to let her lick my mouth. I'd smile and laugh over
the other barking dogs. "She's such a great dog," I'd say, almost
yelling. "So loving and affectionate. The perfect family dog!"

At one point, a mother walked by with her young daughter,
who had long black hair in pigtails and wore a T-shirt with
horses on the front.

Sunny went directly to see the girl, who knelt down at the
bars. "Hola," the girl said, reaching in to pet Sunny. She giggled
when Sunny kissed her hand. The mother, a large, overweight
woman about five feet tall, stood back behind her daughter and
watched with her arms crossed, almost as if bracing herself for
the question. Sunny's tail wagged in frantic circles. "Mommy,
can we take her?" the daughter asked.

The mother's arms fell to her side and she shook her head.
She let out a big sigh. I looked into the mother's eyes and
nodded. I sympathized—wanting to help, wanting to do something, but being powerless.

Sometimes children covered their eyes and ears when walking through the shelter, but this girl pressed her head up against

the bars. She petted Sunny and kissed her and said things in Spanish I couldn't understand. Then I heard her say, "*Te amo,*" and my heart could have melted and sank down the drain along with the pee and dogshit. Why couldn't life be simpler? Why couldn't we help who we loved and keep them safe?

When the mother and daughter walked away, I realized my sadness wasn't the only emotional energy in that kennel. Something about Sunny seemed disappointed, too. She also let out a sigh when she came back into my lap. And I thought how exhausting this must be for a dog like her, one with such a yearning to be near people.

To me, Sunny's behavior conveyed unfailing optimism, as if every person who came by her kennel might be there to let her out, to take her home. But words and human thoughts fail to describe how Sunny wanted to engage with any and everyone, despite whatever cruel things people had done to her in the past. Sunny's body looked half-dead, not only to me but to the older woman who walked by and said, "My God, what happened to her?" and the teenage boy who stared at her and said, "Holy fuckin' shit."

And yet, how alive she was. I had to believe that her liveliness wasn't about a positive attitude or even a social personality but some innate resilience beyond what can be shaped by experience.

38

THE NEXT DAY, I decided to take Sunny out of the kennel. I couldn't take her for a real walk because she wasn't on the high-and-almighty walking list that only an incredibly lucky 10 percent of the dog population was on. (There were so many dogs and only a handful of trainers, and it seemed to take them a long time to approve a dog for walking privileges.)

While I couldn't bring Sunny to the park, I could take her to a small yard at the back of the shelter behind a barred iron gate. Just a few days earlier, I'd taken Mama there, the Rhodesian ridgeback–pit bull mix who'd nearly killed the pigeon I let into her kennel.

Sunny stood still while I wrapped a leash around her neck and opened the kennel door. Dogs barked like crazy all around us. The noise level was deafening, and terrifying to Sunny, who dropped to the ground and began to crawl. Her whole body stayed low and slinking, as if the closer to the earth she was, the safer from all the noise. Some dogs clamped their teeth on the metal bars of their doors and shook them as we walked by. I tried not to look and kept my eyes focused on the slithering dog in front of me.

The small play yard had a white-stained wall on one end filled with tile squares dedicated to well-loved dogs that had passed: "To Fluffy, the best dog that ever lived," and so on. On the other side, behind a few marigold plants, you could see through an old fence to the sidewalk outside of the shelter, where a homeless woman often pushed her grocery cart back and forth, singing "Rock-a-bye-Baby" to herself in a raspy voice, or whistling loud enough to make some dogs perk their ears.

Inside the play yard, there was no grass. Just mulch and dirt and tiny stones. A few water bowls and toys were scattered near a bench held up by two strange bird statues, with eyes that seemed to glow a little and follow you wherever you went. The burning smell of urine was just as bad here as in the kennels, but somehow it felt easier to breathe, as though the sight of a dog off-leash brought more air into the lungs and cleared the eyes and throat.

When I opened the gate and let Sunny free, she promptly christened each bush. Then, as if to say, "*Well, now that that's done,*" she did a glorious, puppy-like play bow, shivering with happiness. She started to run in a circle, her tail wagging in circles, too. The thunderous intensity of such a frail thing shocked me. She looked as though she could have run for miles, but at the same time, this small space, these small circles, seemed enough. She picked up sticks in her mouth and then an old wet stuffed snake toy. Were we anywhere else, I would have encouraged her to put that snake down. Its head looked like it had mold on it.

Instead, I dug in the pockets of my vest to see if I had my phone with me to take a video. When I looked up, a man in his forties wrapped both of his weathered hands around the gate from outside. He wore a black T-shirt with holes, and boots with no shoelaces. Dirt crammed under his fingernails. His hands were wrinkled and tan like his face. His long and straggly hair, a reddish orange color, ran past his shoulders. A tattoo of something I couldn't make out, maybe a dragon, climbed up his neck.

"Nice dog," he said, and Sunny trotted over to meet him. He squatted down so he was eye-level with her and reached in.

"All love, you know?" he said, scratching her chest.

"Yeah."

"If I could take her, I would," the man said. "But I'm home-less myself."

I watched him closely. He was petting Sunny pretty rough. She was a fragile, breakable thing, and he was at least six feet tall.

"I already asked at the front desk," he continued. "You have to fill out all these forms and they do landlord checks and stuff."

"Yeah, they can be pretty strict about that."

"But I'm gonna get off the streets soon. I'm sober now."

He looked up from Sunny when he said those three words: I'm sober now. I had wanted him to leave us alone before those words; I didn't quite trust him. And it wasn't that I trusted him now, but I felt two opposing tides: one pushing me to jump to my feet, open the gate, and hug him for a long time; the other urge, to warn or protect him. To say, "Don't get too cocky. The second you start believing you've got it, that you don't need help anymore, you're fucked."

Instead, I said, "That's a huge deal. Congratulations."

"And once I get a home and my girl comes back to me, things will really get better," he said.

"Well, good luck," I said.

He looked at his bare wrist as if he were wearing a watch and said, "Whoops, I'm late. Gotta go."

Then he looked at Sunny: "You hang in there, okay? You're a good girl."

Sunny peered out the gate and watched him leave, then

trotted back to me, her tail wagging. She lay down, resting her head on my thigh.

"Where do you think he's going?" I asked her. "Where do you think he lives?"

TEN MINUTES AFTER the man left, a volunteer in his sixties, whom I'd last seen patiently attempting to teach Mama the "sit" command, came to the bars. Two leashes were draped around his shoulders and sweat gathered at the top of his balding head. He sighed, probably thankful to have made it down the aisle of barking dogs in one piece, and gave me a half smile.

Since there was only one yard and we needed to share, my time with Sunny was up. He wanted to bring in a blind and deaf husky who was potty-trained and hadn't been out all day, and I couldn't refuse that.

I stood and scanned the yard for where I'd put Sunny's leash, then asked, "So how's Mama been doing?"

The man bit his lower lip and looked down. Then he wiped a bead of sweat from his forehead with the back of his hand, and sighed mournfully.

"She's not with us anymore," he said.

"What?" I said. "Did she get adopted?"

"No . . . the other."

I swallowed hard and looked down at Sunny, who lifted her head in that very same moment, oblivious to the magenta flower petal stuck to her nose.

The petal dropped and she snatched it back up in her mouth, shaking it like a dead animal. I closed my eyes tight, as if that would hold the tears back, but when they opened again, so did the floodgates. The older man looked stricken.

"I know they tried everything to find her a home," he added, his voice soft. "I thought for sure she'd be adopted."

I nodded and cried quietly, unable to speak.

Sometimes in the sun, Mama's coat looked more golden than red, and I had loved petting that coat, loved watching her fetch a ball, loved sitting with her in her kennel. A well-known voice inside told me that Mama's death was my fault, that if I hadn't let that pigeon in her kennel, she'd still be here.

You fucked everything up for her, I thought.

SUNNY ARMY-CRAWLED BY my side as we made our way back to her kennel. She didn't fight me when I locked her in the pen, just sat there at the bars with her nose pushed through like she always did.

I knelt down before her, thinking about how I was going home to sleep in the comfort of a warm bed, leaving Sunny in the same shitty place where Mama had spent her last days.

Sunny leaned her body toward me for petting. She kissed my face and my hands, snorting a bit and wagging her tail.

Filled to the rim again, the bowl shined behind her in the light.

39

AFTER HEARING OF Mama's death, I took a break from the shelter for a few days. During that time, I finally sent a letter to my father. It was an awkward and short letter, but it said that I loved him, and that's the main thing I wanted him to know.

I returned to the shelter early on a Wednesday eager to see Sunny. The next day, I'd be flying to Oregon for a ten-day writers retreat, so I wanted to say goodbye and tell her I'd be back soon.

A stream of yellow pee ran down the side of Sunny's kennel and I sat as far away from it as possible. Sunny sprawled across my lap and I stroked her coat, counting the rigid bones of her spine. She began to snore loudly, sounding so much like a human that I pulled out my cell phone and unsuccessfully tried to record the sound.

I sighed and kissed Sunny's head. "How do you feel, Sunny girl?"

She opened her eyes and lifted her head at the sound of the question, her nostrils pulsing while she sniffed the air.

Then, to my surprise, her muzzle found its way to my pocket. I pulled out a treat and held a small piece of it in front of her nose. Her body tensed. She lifted one paw and set it down, nails scraping against the concrete. Then she got up from my lap and sat in front of me, our faces less than a foot apart.

I sat there frozen, hand extended. So consciously it seemed, she slurped her wet tongue against my skin and swallowed the treat in a single gulp. I imagined it moving down her throat and landing in her empty stomach with a plop, the sound echoing off her bony rib cage. Then she stared at the pockets of my apron, wanting more.

I was stunned. I pulled out another treat and this time she chewed, and then treat after treat, she kept chewing.

I STAYED WITH Sunny for more than an hour that day, until the sun blazed high and the air was so hot that the swirls of cement on the walls started to look like tangible things: birds, elephants, human faces. I stayed with my girl and held her close, my brave girl that was eating again.

Sunny snoozed in my lap after devouring the treats, and my eyes fell on the puppy across the aisle. He was a brindle pit bull, twelve weeks old, with a lime-green bandanna around his neck. The shelter staff often put bandannas and decorative collars on the dogs to make them look more attractive to potential adopters.

This pup had a lean body for a puppy rather than that plump, wrinkly look. He was intently watching a pigeon hobble down the aisle when a leaf, green as his bandanna, flew inside his kennel. His gaze shifted from the bird to the leaf. His eyes bulged—he was completely captivated by it. The leaf spun and twirled in the air just above him, taking its sweet time on its journey down to the ground. I imagined invisible hands tossing the leaf back and forth just over the pup's head. He stood on his hind legs and swatted, to no avail.

Then finally, the leaf hit the ground. The pup exploded with excitement. He play-bowed and barked at the leaf as if it might bark back. The wind blew the leaf a little to the left or to the right and he chased and pawed at it, tail wagging, completely enthralled.

Water poured through the pipe in the wall to clean the floors yet again. The leaf was picked up by the stream and he splashed around following it. He snatched it in his mouth and shook the leaf like crazy. Then he trotted around the width of the kennel in the shallow water, a victory lap.

In the middle of all this suffering, here he was, free.

40

IN THE TOWN of Forest Grove, Oregon, the great oaks and birches scattered around Pacific University were the tallest trees I'd ever seen, some seventy feet high. Early in the mornings before writing classes and workshops started, I found myself looking up at them far more often than at the campus grounds, which with their manicured flower beds, sparkly sidewalks, and freshly cut lawns, were almost too perfect, too clean.

But the treetops were too high to be tamed by human hands. Tangled branches and green leaves grew in every which direction. Sometimes, when white pearly light broke through the clouds and spread across clusters of leaves that seemed more a part of the sky than the earth, I stopped breathing. I almost felt the need to bow to that giant and mysterious and unreachable world of its own, that gorgeous mess.

I wandered beneath those majestic canopies for ten, sometimes twenty minutes, until I arrived at Maggie's Buns, an eclectic, wildly colorful café just off campus. The side of the building was painted in retro-colored stripes, and inside, the walls were lime green with a sky blue ceiling. The place always smelled like cinnamon sticky buns, for which it was famous. Funky trinkets and coffee mugs were scattered about, along with random posters of tomatoes and 1950s ads. The owner, an outgoing, middle-aged woman named Maggie, often greeted me with a warm hug and smile.

I usually sat down near the front window, beside a glass cow figurine, a plastic gorilla, and a hot pink vase of fake sunflowers. After I slabbed some cream cheese onto my bagel and sipped some much-needed coffee, my intention was to fill my blank journal with tales of Big Girl and Mama and all the dogs I hadn't been able to save, if just for the sake of putting on paper that they existed, that their lives were not meaningless.

Perhaps, beneath that intention, was the secret belief that my suffering didn't compare to their suffering, and was therefore less important. I felt an urgent need to tell the stories of shelter dogs—for their lives not to be forgotten, for their voices to be heard.

But day after day on a purple table at Maggie's Buns, I found that a lusty high schooler needed to be heard, too. And a college student holding on to hope for her dad's sobriety. And a so-called adult who didn't know what to do with the food in her stomach or the pain in her heart. I found that before I could write about any tail wags or belly rubs, these voices needed to speak first. They demanded room on white lined paper.

I found that I had to write about where obsession lived. Where rituals were born. Where a girl believed that sucking in her stomach made her more beautiful, more vital, more seen in the world. I had to write about where she got those beliefs.

I had to write about Brad Michaels, a popular, pot-smoking, Dave Matthews–loving guy I met shortly after I became bulimic. He had a smile that made girls want to rip their bras off. His face was a mouthwatering kind of handsome, his body ripples of muscle.

He had never paid much attention to me in high school, but

after I dropped some weight and got a new wardrobe, he flirted with me at a party. A few nights later we went on a date to the movies, where our legs were excruciatingly close together in the dark. I looked down at them far more than I looked up at the screen. When he placed his hand on my thigh, a jolt of electricity ran through my body so fast I could have passed out.

Brad and I went back to his parents' big house, which I think was made of brick, but then again, I rarely saw it in daylight. On the couch in the living room, Brad felt me up while *Saturday Night Live* played in the background. He said my legs were the smoothest he'd ever touched, and I said nothing because if I opened my mouth, I would have screamed, "I love you!"

I kept my hands cautiously away from his pants, not wanting to look like an idiot since I didn't know how to give a hand or blow job yet. The game now was to pretend I wasn't terrified. But of course, it wasn't a game at all. I wanted Brad to want me more than I'd ever wanted anything in my life. When he held my hand, I felt the eyes of other girls on me, wishing Brad Michaels was holding *their* hand, wishing Brad Michaels was pouring *them* a drink. The attention filled me up, buffet-style.

ONE FRIDAY NIGHT at a house party, Brad sat on a bed and I knelt down before him. I kissed his lips, then took off my yellow sundress to buy myself a little time. I knew what he wanted, something I'd failed to do multiple times before. He pushed my head down into his crotch. I froze and gasped an anxious breath. Why couldn't I just do it already? What the hell was wrong with me?

My fingers fumbled around the zipper. When I couldn't get it to move, I placed my hands on his knees.

"Sorry," I said.

"I can't fuckin' do this," he said.

He couldn't fuckin' do this?

By the anger in his voice, I almost expected Brad to spit on me. He was done. Over my shit. He stood up and stormed out of the bedroom, the door slamming behind him, the Red Sox cap that had hung on the knob falling to the floor.

Whenever I feel intense emotion, I feel it in my throat, like choking on a sharp rock. The carpet vibrated beneath my bare feet to the bass of an Eminem song. My esophagus stung with tears. Through the window, holding my dress over my chest, I watched Brad walk across a front yard covered in empty beer cans, probably in search of a girl who wasn't terrified of going down on him, or more accurately, going down and doing it wrong.

"Fuck him," I said, snapping the blinds shut.

And then I went home and did just that.

I fucked him the way I fucked anyone I didn't like. I fucked him by gorging on gallons of ice cream and digging my hands into cold lasagna. I fucked him by taking my fury out on the fridge and eating my fears out of my mother's pantry.

The kitchen was eerily dark, the granite countertops wiped clean and reeking of 409, the walls covered with pictures of my sister and me. The only light came from inside the fridge. Food pacified me, made me stronger. I could step out of my life and into a cake, without a single all-consuming thought of my inadequacy. The food didn't need me to be cool, to dress up and look good, to say the right thing, to do the right thing with a boy's dick.

Bingeing was the opposite of prettiness and perfection. It was rude, gluttonous, sinful—a giant middle finger to the strict, calorie-conscious rules I abided by during the day. Some of my friends ate like me. Dieting was the thing. We aimed for Britney Spears bodies. We threw up. We worked out for hours trying to make our flat stomachs even flatter. A rumbling stomach was a sign that we were doing good, we were on our way.

In the bathroom, I flipped up the toilet seat. While pulling my hair back, I heard a bump and then another against a wall. I heard mumbled gibberish. My father. He was stumbling down the hallway.

Dad tripped over something and fell. I heard him gripping the kitchen counter, slowly steadying himself back onto his feet.

I leaned over the toilet bowl, shoved my hands down my throat, and puked.

I HAD TO write about one winter break in college, when I came home and went with Dad to a cold church basement. Drunks trying to get or stay sober gathered there. We made our way into a room that felt sort of like a cave and smelled like burnt coffee. Everyone was bundled up in jackets, and some still wore their gloves and scarves. People hugged my father for long moments and whispered, "Glad you're here," into his ear. He nodded and looked down a lot. I think he had been sober for about two weeks.

We sat down at one end of a long table with ten or fifteen chairs around it. White Styrofoam cups filled with coffee shook in hands that couldn't stay still. A homeless man with yellow teeth and chapped lips sat across from Dad, and he started off the meeting with a prayer.

Then a book that looked like a blue Bible was passed around the table, and when it got to my father, I studied his face . . . its authenticity, its vulnerability. He read a passage about surrender, about how people have faith in all kinds of things without questioning it, like electricity, and even in their own minds. The book suggested trying to have faith in Something greater than yourself, which, unlike booze, would never let you down.

I'd never seen my dad as nervous as I did during that meeting, but I could hear it in his voice when he read, in the way he stumbled over some words. When he passed the book to the next alcoholic, he did so in a reluctant way, as if he didn't want to see it go.

Throughout the meeting, people "shared." Some held back tears, but their lips still quivered with emotion. Some had lost their family, homes, jobs, and freedom. All of them had lost their confidence and dignity. Even when their every intention was to run from the drink, for some crazy reason, they drew closer.

They spoke of a disease that took everything. One bald, old man with a cane said, "The most insane thing I ever did wasn't to drink and drive. It wasn't to rob a bank. It was to take that goddamn sip of alcohol again, knowing all the chaos and pain it would bring."

"I'm insane!" a woman with short red hair and a puffy black jacket said. "I do the one thing that hurts me again and again. My mind is the problem. Alcohol is just a symptom."

Part of me sat at the edge of my seat, recognizing this talk of insanity, of what a horrible thing it was to be scared of your own self. But another part of me thought: *Shit, you people need some help.*

On the drive home from the meeting, Dad blared his music like he always had when I was growing up. We rolled down the windows despite the cold air and shouted out lyrics to the Counting Crows. We drove through random neighborhoods just to see their Christmas lights, just to sing a little longer. I took my boots off and put my feet on the dashboard. His car was spotless except for his gym bag on the floor under my legs. It was unzipped and I could see the mouthwash, cologne, and hairspray he doused himself in before he came home, often to cover up the scent of alcohol seeping from his pores.

I let myself believe there would be nothing to cover up this Christmas. I let myself believe that the smile on his face, and the clarity in his eyes, were here to stay.

When we pulled into the driveway, he turned the music down and looked over at me. "I've hit rock bottom, honey," he said. "I really have this time. Everything's about to change for the better."

But the next night, on Christmas Eve, he was wasted. We found him in my parents' bedroom, his body limp, eyes rolling to the back of his head.

Back to rehab he went.

I HAD TO write about how, like my father, I hit rock bottom so many times I almost came to believe it was my second home. But each nosedive into food and vomit chipped away at the idea that I could handle things by myself, and sometimes it frightened me into action.

Shortly after I moved to San Diego, I went to a beach in La Jolla around 2 A.M. No public restrooms were open and I'd just devoured a pizza, so I crouched down in the sand to throw it up. The ink-black water and a few homeless people were my only company. The cloudy sky looked like an ugly blanket choking a cluster of stars, dimming their light.

I puked until my stomach churned and a puddle of vomit stared back at me in the sand. Then I licked my chapped lips and wiped my hands on my yoga pants, turning around to go back to my car.

A woman came out from behind a large palm tree, startling me so much that I fell to the ground. I looked up at her face and realized that she wasn't there to rob or rape me. She was in her forties or fifties with blond hair, wearing blue jeans, and a Save the Earth T-shirt.

"Please, don't walk past the white rope," she said. She pointed farther down the beach. Someone, probably her, had strung a rope near the seals to prevent people from getting too close.

What I wanted to say was that I loved those seals as much as she did. I loved how they curled up in heart-shaped shadows on the rocks and slept inside gentle waves and nursed their babies on the beaches.

"Sorry," I mumbled, barely able to face the woman. Fire burned in my throat. The stench and heat of my self-hatred was all-consuming.

The woman gave me an eerie smile before she walked away, a smile that said, *I know your secrets. I know you're not who you say you are.*

I walked down to the ocean. The frigid water and the dead things it carried, rocks and shards of seashells, brushed up against my ankles. The moon stayed hidden behind the fog while I aimlessly wandered along the shore, my heart heavy, my feet numb.

The first call I made to Rosewood was the next morning, curled up in my bed, sand still on my feet, vomit still on my breath.

"I'm scared of myself," I said to the operator.

She connected me to the Intake Department.

BY THE TIME I flew out of Portland, I hadn't written about Big Girl or Mama or a single shelter dog. Instead, I left with pages of boys I thought never mattered, pizzas I puked, beers I chugged, fears I ran from, secrets I kept, dead things I felt.

And when I arrived back in San Diego, I surprisingly loved those coffee-stained, Maggie's Buns pages. I loved them even if they were overly sentimental and confusing and probably not very "good." I loved them because for once I had written what I needed to write, instead of what I believed I was supposed to write.

I loved them because they were a gorgeous mess.

My gorgeous mess.

41

IN LATE JUNE, I returned from Oregon and walked down the first row of kennels at the shelter. A pit bull with a dirty white coat, freckles on her tongue, and a mournful look in her green eyes stared back at me from her pen. Red, pin-size holes spread across the top of her head and the tips of her ears. Was it some kind of rash? A chemical burn?

"It's the flies," someone said from behind me. I turned around to face a staff member in a brown jumpsuit whom I often saw cleaning the kennels and feeding the animals. He was black and short with an Afro, a kid, I guessed, maybe sixteen.

"The flies?" I asked.

"They always pick on the ones with the thick heads. Feast on them every summer."

I reached through the bars, moving my hands from the dog's chest to her head. The holes were deeper than I thought. They painted fresh blood on my fingertips.

"Shit," I said. Then I turned back to the kid. "Sorry, I just haven't seen this before."

He wore a thin black cord with headphones around his neck, a faint beat blaring through them. "Don't have to censor yourself around me," he said. "Do you know how many times a day

I say 'shit'? I fucking clean shit." Then he started to unwind a hose from a reel on the side of the kennel to do just that.

The walkie-talkie buckled to his jumpsuit belt started buzzing. He stared at the white dog for a second and tossed a treat in her kennel, then hurried to the front office.

The dog gobbled up the treat and looked at me for more. I tossed a few in her kennel and then headed to the back corner of the shelter. I was in a hurry to see my girl, and I rushed to the kennel where she'd been for the past month. But when I got there, she was gone. Replaced by two Chihuahuas trembling in the back corner of the kennel instead.

I nearly ran to the front office, passing a shelter employee who worked in the Development Department and was kissing dog after dog through the bars. Her red lipstick was smeared on her chin. I rushed past two Humane Investigations officers and a young family. All I could think about was how I had let Sunny down, how I should have been there, how I should have adopted her myself.

In the main office, I pushed past a young guy inquiring about surrendering his cat and cut the line of customers waiting at the front desk. I stepped up to the counter and gripped its ledge to steady myself.

"Hi. A one-year-old relinquished pit bull in kennel seventy-two, Sunny, K818104," I said. "Was she adopted?"

A girl in her twenties with frizzy hair looked up from her keyboard. If she had told me to wait in line, I'd have had a mental breakdown, and maybe she sensed that. She pounded the digits into the keyboard. Her forehead wrinkled and she moved close to the screen as if to see better. Then she looked up at me.

"She's on the euthanasia list," she said.

I gasped and lurched over the counter to see the computer screen. I wanted to see the words; I wanted confirmation.

The girl pinched her lips together. "If she's not in her kennel, it probably happened today."

I dropped my face into my hands and started weeping, inconsolable. A stranger put his hand on my back as a gesture of comfort, which made me cry harder.

The girl closed her eyes, green just like the white pit bull's eyes had been. When she opened them, she said, "I'm sorry. We have been having a lot of space issues."

"Are you sure?" I sobbed.

She nodded, looking behind me to the next customer, like she didn't have time for this.

"Can I have the bathroom key?" I asked. My throat was a salt marsh of tears. "Please?"

She opened a drawer and pulled out a red braided rope toy, attached to a tiny key. I grabbed the key and pushed through the office door, walking down a row of kennels to the bathroom. I wanted to sprint but my body wouldn't let me. Each step sluggish and dizzying. Heat rose to my face. The wind blew strong against me. The sky was dim but not yet raining. The more dogs I passed, the more shiny red heads I saw. Most of them were pit bulls. None of them were Sunny.

But then, as I was about to turn right to the bathroom, I saw a familiar muzzle pushing through the jagged bars of a kennel. I choked on my breath. I stopped and stared at a black, fat nose, with a cluster of white fur at the tip of the muzzle and long black whiskers. The dog was standing on three legs, resting her fourth paw, the right front one, on a horizontal bar across the kennel door. Three toes had white fur and the others were gray. I knew that muzzle. And I knew that paw. I'd held it many times before.

This was Sunny. I stepped up to the kennel. The bars were so bent she could almost fit her entire head through one of the openings. Sunny wore a filthy and faded pink collar, and she looked horrible, like she had lost ten pounds. She jumped up on her hind legs and put both paws on the bars, whimpering, her screw tail going wild. I wrapped my hands around the bars, hung my head over her muzzle, kissed her face, and choked on my breath and tears.

"I'm so sorry," I cried. "I'm so, so sorry."

I unlocked the kennel and bent down to the ground while the door slammed shut behind me. Sunny nestled into my lap as a terrified child might. Four flies swarmed around her and I swatted at them constantly. There were two clumps of red holes by each of her floppy ears. Blood gathered there and glistened in the sunlight. I touched her head. She winced and stood up.

Sunny would lie in my lap for just a minute or so, then get up and go to the front of the cage, jumping up on her hind legs. She had a restlessness that was new and powerful, a restlessness I couldn't soothe. The flies seemed to be only a small part of it.

Down she lay, then up again. Down, then up. For the next twenty minutes. What had comforted me in the past was how quickly Sunny fell asleep in my lap. She'd collapse on my legs, falling asleep like she hadn't slept in days, snoring, and I could tell myself that at least I was giving her some rest.

Now I couldn't seem to give her that comfort, but clearly, almost immaculately, I knew what she gave me.

When I was around Sunny, there was no time to dream about some easier, prettier, more comprehensible, less fucked-up existence. Now was all we had: Sunny lifting her eyes to meet mine. Cupping water in my own hands to rinse the blood off her head. Sunny's tongue on my nose, her tail thudding on my leg. The reach of my hand across her spine. The words of comfort and rage and fear and sadness and hope that I spoke only in her presence.

When I was around Sunny, I looked closer. I studied the color of her paws (gray and white) and the color of her eyes (chestnut, reflecting my face in them) and the pace of her breath (hurried, restless). I wasn't lost in my head, blind to the beauty or the suffering in front of me.

When I was around Sunny, wearing filthy jeans and my face covered in slobber, I was the kind of person I wanted to be.

Sunny came back into my lap. I grazed my hand along her back. I held her paw. I looked into her tired eyes.

"Your life matters," I said.

A mother and her daughter, who was maybe five years old, came by. Sunny got up and went to the front of the bars and pushed her muzzle through. Her ears shifted and twitched in the air thick with dust. Then Sunny let out a sudden, high-pitched bark.

Startled, the little girl backed away, looking from Sunny then to me, and asked, "Mommy, why is everyone here crying?"

She was talking about the shelter dogs and me.

RESCUE GROUPS ARE often run by volunteers who donate their time and financial resources to take in animals on euthanasia lists or rescue them from other dire situations. These incredible people foster and care for the animals until a permanent home can be found for them, often paying for the animal's medical expenses and helping them to grow as behaviorally and physically healthy as possible for their new family. Some shelters have a designated employee who reaches out to rescue groups in an attempt to save animals from euthanasia.

I knew that the rescue coordinator for this shelter, Lisa, cared deeply about the animals. She worked tirelessly on their behalf, but she was only one person, and she could only do so much.

So after thirty minutes with Sunny, I went to my car to give Lisa a call. With Sunny's hair all over my jeans, I dialed her number from the shelter's parking lot, and I lied.

I said I had a rescue group interested in Sunny, and I just needed a few days to work out the details. I also said that if the rescue group fell through, I would adopt Sunny myself.

Danny and I had already gotten into a big fight over adopting Sunny, even before the news that her life was on the line. While Bella did well with other dogs in public, she became very territorial in our apartment, which she considered her domain. Danny thought another dog would stress her out too much, and that it just wasn't the right time in our lives. I knew that he was right, but I didn't want to admit it.

Lisa didn't need to know this. What she needed to know was that I was determined to rescue Sunny. By the end of the phone call, Lisa said she couldn't remove Sunny from the euthanasia list, but she could let staff know that there was a potential lead for a rescue group or adoption.

Then she told me to call her when I had more information.

If nothing else, I had bought Sunny time.

42

OVER THE NEXT few days, Sunny looked more miserable every time I visited. Her bones threatened to break through the skin, so sharp and defined inside that frail body not even a year old. Specks of blood covered the crown of her head and the tips of her silver, floppy ears. The stench that rose up from her oily coat smelled like something dying. In fact, the whole shelter smelled like it was on its way out of this world.

Sunny was never happy when I left her kennel, but now she threw herself up against the bars in protest when I would leave. The cage rattled and her whimpers echoed down the aisle—nightmarish sounds I began to hear in my dreams. They reminded me of the squeaky wheelchairs down the hallway at Rosewood, the clanking of forks on plates, the weeping that went on during meals.

My life became a quest to get Sunny out of danger. I began by doing what any emotionally charged animal lover might do, making a video of Sunny to sentimental music and blasting it to every friend I had on Facebook, along with a picture of her behind bars with a tagline that said, "She doesn't have much time. Help her find a home."

I used the video I took when I was trying to capture the

sound of her snoring. She lay in my lap, flies swarming her face, my hand constantly batting them away. She looked peaceful and content, but also like any other shelter dog. How could I show people she was so much more?

I called more than forty rescue groups and emailed the ones I could with the video. I reached out to the TV stations I used to work with in San Diego, but stumbled over my words, unable to explain to producers why Sunny should be rescued when so many healthy and loving dogs were euthanized in Los Angeles every day. I talked about how she had begun to eat again and the moment she dunked her head in water, but none of it could get at her toughness, her thirst for life.

All I knew was that I couldn't let Sunny share Big Girl's and Mama's fate. It was against volunteer policy to reach out to the media and post self-made videos online, but I didn't care.

Seeing Sunny's body begin to heal in that cage—it did something to me. I'd known dozens of dogs who were euthanized before and I never handled it well. But if Sunny were put down, some essential part of me would be put down, too. Losing her meant losing my ability to recover from something vague but deep. My faith. My authenticity. My hope.

So many dogs became mentally and physically ill in the shelter. They were locked in pens without access to the sights, sounds, and smells of the earth that made them feel alive and made them feel like dogs. Some of the dogs that were calm on day one would be gnawing on the metal bars by day three. Dogs who were once all eagerness and play would sleep at the back of their kennels, unwilling to lift their heads. I kept waiting for Sunny to lose her deep yearning for human connection, but she didn't.

Every time I walked down her row of kennels, there was that wet, black nose pushing through the bars. She was so different from me and most people I knew—we tend to hide when life gets hard. We're afraid to love, afraid to even ask for help. All I wanted during those long nights vomiting was to be left the fuck alone.

Not Sunny girl.

Deep down within, there was power and resilience. She wanted to do more than survive. She pushed her muzzle through jagged bars and called out for a better life. She called out for love.

Not cupcakes. Not vodka. Not isolation. Not death.

But love.

And I could not just move on with my life and pretend I never heard that brave call.

43

ANOTHER THING VOLUNTEERS weren't supposed to do was bring cell phones into the kennels with the dogs. But days after I called Lisa, I still hadn't found a rescue group to take Sunny, and I was about to break out of the shelter with her in my arms, or chain myself to Sunny's kennel the way some people chain themselves to trees, so none of the rules mattered anymore.

My grandma Elsie has an alarm in her heart that goes off every time I need her. That's the only way I can explain it, how she always calls me when I'm convinced there is no hope and everything's gone to shit. Which is exactly how I felt as Sunny paced around me, refusing to take the kibble and water I offered to her with cupped hands. It was as though Sunny knew I was going to leave her again, and that her time was running out.

My phone vibrated in the pocket of my volunteer apron and "Grandma Elsie" lit up the screen.

At the sound of my voice, Grandma said, "Honey, what's going on?"

I hadn't yet told her about Sunny, but I'd told her about the shelter dogs, and having raised six children, five foster children, and God knows how many animals on a farm, and having lived eighty-plus years in this world, she knew that no pain was ever to be discounted. She knew all of us needed to be heard at times, all of us needed to be rescued.

"I'm in a kennel with this dog, Sunny," I said. "And she's on the euthanasia list and I love her and she's such a good dog."

I went on to ask her all the questions spinning around my mind. Why did my dreams matter more than Sunny's dreams? Because I was human? Because I can say the word *dreams*? Who was to say that Sunny's love wouldn't save a life? Who was to say that her unique body and mind and heart weren't made to do something extraordinary?

"Honey," Grandma Elsie said. "The longer I live the more questions I don't have answers to. Life is so sad. Some things are worse than death. But you can hold her now. You can love her."

I held the phone up against my ear with my shoulder, and dipped my hands into Sunny's bowl of lukewarm water. I stroked my wet fingers along her back and the top of her head in a hopeless effort to keep her cool.

Then Grandma said, "When I lost your grandpa and Diane, what helped me the most were the little things. Your mom cooking supper. My grandbaby giving me a smile. Some stranger being nice to me at my job. Little things are actually big things. Sometimes they're everything," she said.

I WANTED TO believe Grandma Elsie. I wanted to believe that the simplest, most ordinary things could be lifesaving. I wanted to believe that every act of love and kindness, however small, mattered in a cosmically big way.

But as I continued to come up empty-handed for Sunny, something inside me was shutting down. I had worked hard over the years to cultivate an awareness that life was not all-or-nothing, good or bad, black or white. I had worked hard to see through to the fallacy of *Fuck It* thinking: *I ate this much, so fuck it, I might as well eat the rest of the cake. I puked once, so fuck it, I might as well puke again. I'm having a bad day, so fuck it, the whole day is shit.*

But as rescue group after rescue group said no—as Danny and I continued to fight over adopting Sunny—as Sunny remaining in her kennel meant one less space for another homeless dog—the world was quickly becoming nothing, bad, black. It was hard for me to see the beauty in anything, let alone the little things.

Because if a pit bull as loving as Sunny couldn't find a home, then what chance did any pit bull have?

And if I couldn't help Sunny, then fuck it, what was the point in trying to help anyone at all?

44

ALMOST A WEEK after Sunny was condemned to the euthanasia list, my sister more or less forced me to take a break from my rescue efforts, and we went to a local dog park with Bella. Half of the park was covered in dirt, while the other half was healthy and green. There were a few gay couples, two guys with mushroom cuts (which were awful, my sister pointed out), a lot of old, likely retired people, and then of course, all of our dogs. Owners clapped their hands and slapped their thighs and commanded their dogs to come. Some dogs listened, others blatantly ignored the calls. A few looked back curiously before making what seemed like a conscious decision to run in the other direction.

I unleashed Bella, who promptly went nuts, chasing after other dogs, sniffing butts, barking every now and then just for the heck of it, and joyously throwing herself into dead worms and bugs on the ground.

Julie and I sat down at a picnic table, watching Bella and not saying much to each other. A pack of small dogs zoomed past. Bella joined in on the chase, but then switched groups to run with three black Labs that she apparently found more interesting.

"Bella!" I screamed, when one of the sixty-pound Labs leapt

up into the air to snatch a Frisbee and landed about an inch from Bella.

She stopped in her tracks and her chest heaved. Her cream muzzle and even her tongue was covered in red dirt, looking like a baby lifting her head from a plate of pasta.

I took a deep breath. "Jesus, she's got no clue about her size," I said, though of course, sometimes I got confused in that department, too.

ON THE HEALTHY-GRASS side, a beam of sunlight stretched about twenty yards and dyed the hairs of the grass blond. Bella now played in the light with a feather in her mouth. Like Sugar, she enjoyed picking up weightless things, the trick of carrying something but being barely able to feel it.

An obese dachshund walked by with rolls of fat drooping over the ground, almost hiding his legs completely. A few feet away, a boxer shamelessly rolled around in the dirt, treating the earth like his personal backscratcher, all four paws up facing the sky. His lips were rolled back and his teeth showed—it looked like he was grinning.

I forced a smile, but the effort was too much and I looked down. It was the only time in my life I'd ever felt sad at a dog park. Surrounded by so much untamed joy and downright silliness, I couldn't help but think about how unfair it was that these dogs enjoyed such ecstatic freedom, such love and adoration from their owners, just miles from other dogs who were dying in lonely cages. Sunny, and all the dogs at the shelter, seemed so forgotten. So unseen.

Just a few feet from the smiling boxer, I felt overcome by the need to understand why so much cruelty existed in the world. Why so many lives end too soon. I wanted this to be explained and justified to me. Slowly and thoroughly. By the Dalai Lama or Hafiz or Rumi or Thich Nhat Hanh. By someone who could see beyond what I saw. Which was unfairness. Everywhere.

But even if I did receive the explanation I was looking for, would it make the dogs I'd lost and the suffering I'd witnessed okay? Would it ease my pain?

Maybe some things are never okay. Or maybe there's a greater purpose for pain, one that I just wasn't seeing or was unwilling to see.

I sighed heavily enough for my sister to eye me and suggest we get smoothies. I called for Bella, who made her way back to me, while a red pit bull appeared out of nowhere, running toward Julie like he'd known her forever. She dropped to her knees. She didn't care that her black polka-dot dress would get dirty, and she didn't flinch at the dog's large size or at the fact that she didn't know him. He was twenty feet away, then ten, and then there in Julie's arms. She wrapped both arms around the dog and he licked her face and slobbered all over her right ear.

"Doesn't this make you feel like we've got it all wrong?" I said.

"What do you mean?"

"I mean the way we live. We get confused about what's important."

The dog was completely relaxed, basking in the light of Julie's attention, thumping his tail in the dirt. They had the same expression on their faces: mouths slightly open, eyes closed, utterly at ease. I wished I felt that way. I wished the red dog was Sunny.

Julie's glittery, blue nails grazed up and down the dog's back. "Well, some things are important," she said.

Then my sister was laughing louder than I'd heard her laugh in a long time, and the dog was kissing her ear again.

45

THE NEXT DAY, after several more unsuccessful attempts to transfer Sunny out of the shelter, I went to a meeting. Lately, no matter how much I ate, I was still hungry. Addictive craving can erase all your knowledge about how and why food is not the answer, and make you starve for something that will only leave you feeling emptier. I wanted to be around people who understood this, and for them to talk about the sick places they'd been, perhaps as a reminder of why I shouldn't consider visiting them.

But the topic of discussion was love, and someone said that love was the woman that she kissed in bed each morning. Someone said love was doing the thing she didn't want to do, which was to call somebody for help instead of eating three pizzas at midnight. Someone said love was prayer. Someone said love is the thing we're all searching for. Someone said love is everywhere.

I believed there was a lot less love in the world than anybody in this room claimed. I thought about Sunny and her time running out. I thought about all the dogs I had known whose time had already run out. I felt angry and separate from the people I normally identified with to the core.

·   ·   ·

WHEN THE MEETING was over, a bulimic soccer mom held the front door open for a teenage suicide attempt survivor and then me. In the parking lot, two college students walked on either side of an obese woman who made her clothing out of sheets. An anorexic mother pulled out her gym bag from the trunk of her BMW. Linda and Rayna, a couple in their thirties, waved at me while they drove past in a blue minivan.

The sun shone down on the parking lot behind two pearly cumulus clouds. I leaned against the wall of the building and dialed the Humane Society's main office.

The person who answered the phone did not share the same enthusiasm that everyone else I encountered had about Sunny. "Listen, we've done all we can," she said to me after I gave her Sunny's ID number, and then hung up.

In truth, this girl probably loved animals and worked at a shelter because she wanted to help them, but Los Angeles's overwhelming stray population was a reality she had to face five days a week. Still, I was ready to rip her a new one.

But when I called back, no one picked up. The Humane Society's website wasn't loading on my phone. I kept hitting reload, expecting to find Sunny's picture removed from the list of dogs available for adoption.

When I looked up, a short, three-hundred-pound woman in her fifties stood before me. She wore white sneakers, and a flower muumuu, and smelled like men's deodorant. Her name was Sally, and she'd heard me talk about Sunny during the meeting. She placed her fat, pale hands on my shoulders.

"You know, if she's put down, at least she won't be suffering anymore," she said.

I closed my eyes tight and then opened them, clenching my phone in one hand and a Forever 21 receipt with Sunny's information on the back in the other. Sally had a gap between her two front teeth and her breath smelled like cheese. She wore a beaded bracelet that spelled out the word SERENITY.

"She won't have to live another day in that kennel you described," she continued. Then Sally hugged me tight, the heat of her body pressed against my chest.

"I'm sorry," she whispered into my ear, petting my hair.

I knew Sally wasn't the one I was mad at, but I honestly could have slapped her across the face. She was acting like it was over. Like Sunny was already gone. And almost, like it was a good thing.

My arms wouldn't lift to hug her back. I felt the rigid edges of bad things happening to good creatures and the impossibility of understanding why crammed into my chest. *Fuck you*, I wanted to say. The air around us was hot, unforgiving, and I was swallowing it, gulping it down. Maybe I was even panting.

"Sweetie, she's going to be okay," Sally said, finally letting me go.

"But that's what I told her and it's a lie. She's not okay."

Sally touched the rim of her glasses and looked up at the sky as though she was thinking hard. "I'm not sure if lying is the same as believing you have more control than you do."

There was a gentle breeze. Then Sally pinched her lips together. "But I can tell you one thing, honey," she said. "It hurts just as bad."

SALLY GOT INTO her station wagon and lowered the body of the car with her weight. I pulled out of the parking lot behind her and stopped at a light. A copper lotus flower necklace hung from my rearview mirror and looked bright yellow in the sun.

"Do you know where lotus flowers bloom from?" Danny had asked when he gave it to me years earlier. I'd shaken my head while he clasped the chain around my neck. "The mud, honey. They bloom from the mud," he'd said.

I used to touch that flower when in the crux of my eating disorder. I also used to keep things like a notecard with the Serenity Prayer and a photo of my sister taped to my dashboard, last-ditch attempts to keep me from turning to the food. My car was the place I binged the most.

When the light turned green, Sally waved out of the window and turned left and I was suddenly starving. I'd already eaten lunch, but what I was experiencing now wasn't physical hunger. It was soul hunger.

The rationalizing began almost as soon as traffic picked up. I could have one extremely early dinner and not eat the rest of the day. I could go to yoga and work it all off that night . . .

BEFORE I KNEW it, I'd pulled into McDonald's, which was like stopping at a bar after an AA meeting. I just wanted soothing comfort. I wanted to exit from anxiety and enter beefy oblivion. Then I wanted to make myself hollow as a drum.

My mouth was salivating. My hands, like a drug addict's, trembled in anticipation of the food. It had been close to three years since the last time I'd done this, but that didn't cross my mind.

I was about to order three Big Macs and lie to the cashier about how two of the Big Macs were for Danny and run to the nearest bathroom and stick my hands down my throat and vomit like I'd never stopped. I was about to begin that vicious cycle, which may or may not have landed me back in treatment or worse.

But my phone rang. It was like an alarm in the passenger's seat, waking me from a dream. The fact that it might have been a rescue group was the only reason I picked up. There was just one car in front of me to the drive-thru menu.

It was Alicia Stevenson, the founder of Project Unleashed. I'd contacted her the day before, having heard that Project Unleashed brought rescue dogs into prisons to rehabilitate the youth there. The dogs were all rescued from shelters and mostly pit bulls. They did this important prison work until Alicia could find them a permanent home.

"If it's not too late, we'll rescue her," Alicia said.

My hands gripped the wheel and I made a sharp turn out of the drive-thru line. I parked by a palm tree in the back of the lot and immediately called the shelter.

When I got through, I found out that my girl was still alive. What happened in my chest was some kind of an explosion, the same feeling I once got when I avoided a major car crash by a millisecond. I wanted to scream, I wanted to weep, but instead I sat quietly in the pink neon glare of an "Open 24 Hrs." sign and told myself to breathe.

A few surfer dudes ran past, then a young couple walking two Dalmatians.

A little girl with braids in her hair skipped across the parking lot and into McDonald's.

46

SOMETIMES, YOU HAVE to learn a lesson more than once, and I had learned yet again that reaching out when you're struggling is courageous, not weak. I had admired Sunny all along for pushing her muzzle through the bars of her cage—now I saw the value and the beauty of doing it myself.

During the week after Sunny's rescue, I called my therapist and several people from my recovery group, both in San Diego and Los Angeles. I went to a meeting every day, and in simply speaking up and asking for help, the desire to binge left me. I began to feel like myself again, a girl who believed in the beauty of small, ordinary things.

Alicia called me shortly after Sunny arrived in her care, and she said that Sunny looked healthier every day. Alicia was the daughter of two Broadway actors, and by day she worked in Hollywood on sound effects for movies. On nights and weekends, she worked with shelter dogs and incarcerated youth through Project Unleashed.

Sunny got along great with Alicia's six miracle dogs, each one of them having been rescued and adopted by Alicia after surviving unthinkable circumstances: fifteen years of confinement in a small cage; dogfighting; intentional starvation; horrific abuse. While some still showed signs of trauma, all of them embraced the long-awaited love and freedom they found in Alicia's home.

Alicia said that I was welcome to meet the gang anytime, and that it would be wonderful for me to see how well Sunny was doing in person. I couldn't resist the offer.

RESCUE GROUPS WORK with minimal funds, so I was surprised when Alicia gave me an address in Malibu. I drove up a mountaintop along the Pacific Ocean, passing one tall wrought-iron gate after another. The views of the water, forest, and wildflowers were straight out of a travel brochure. I rolled my windows down and the scent of ocean air traveled all the way up the mountains.

Alicia's boyfriend, Chip, buzzed me into the property. I drove down a gravel driveway with trees bending inward on either side, forming a green ceiling.

When a quaint blue home came into view, so did Sunny. She sat at Chip's side on a leash, and I could already tell she had gained weight. I pulled up to them and Sunny leapt up on her hind legs and placed her front paws on my window. She stretched her neck and nudged her head as far as possible into my car, her body warm and looking remarkably stronger. I held the weight of her head in my hands and kissed her profusely, tasting grass on her muzzle and gazing into her eyes.

Once Sunny and I had thoroughly loved on each other, Chip pointed to the end of the driveway and told me to park my car there. When I stepped outside, Sunny came running from a distance. My back pressed against the front door of my car and I slid down, squatting with my arms open wide. At the rate of her sprinting, it looked like she might crash into me, but then at just a few feet away she slowed and gently nestled her head under my legs, her whole body wiggling back and forth with that stub tail wagging behind her.

When she raised her head and licked my face, I realized that the specks of blood were gone. She had on a new, clean black collar. Her coat smelled like soap and butter. The sound of her panting was all I could hear, plus a few chirping birds.

My God, I thought. *Where are we, girl?*

I followed Sunny to a long deck at the back of the house. Sunlight spread across it, giving the wood a pale yellow glow. Sunny jumped into a plush, chestnut-colored dog bed and rolled on her back, her black lips flipped upside down. Through the glass windows of the home, I saw a thin and shy-looking pit bull standing beside a much heftier and goofier one, an old but curious hound mix, and a German shepherd mix playing with a chew toy. I assumed Chip had left the rest of the dogs inside so Sunny and I could have alone time.

When Chip joined us, he gazed at Sunny lovingly. Chip was slim, about my height and in his thirties, and I immediately sensed a kind presence. He told me that he was a documentarian, and like Alicia, he was very involved with helping the incarcerated youth in Los Angeles.

Both of us scratched Sunny's belly and cooed at her. Her belly was full and her body relaxed. Chip pointed to her stub tail thudding on the wood, "So do you know what happened there?"

"Part of me doesn't want to know," I said.

He nodded and sighed. "She's still hesitant. Constantly looking up at Alicia and me as if to ask if she can go into a room, or go outside like the other dogs, like she's never sure if it's okay. And she's really weird around food. Sometimes she gobbles it down. Sometimes she won't touch it."

With one hand on her rib cage and the other under her chin, I leaned down and kissed my girl on her muzzle. "I don't blame her," I said.

AN HOUR LATER, Alicia was running late from work, and Sunny and I were alone in a secluded yard behind the house. But not just any yard, one with rocking chairs, a hammock, a hot tub, toys, rawhides, and a small pond. There was no concrete. No ticking clock. Nothing but nature, untouched and majestic. Despite so many days in a pen, Sunny knew exactly what to do, exactly how to enjoy her freedom.

She dove into the pond with an unapologetic splash. Later I'd learn that even the fish there were rescued, and I smiled at the thought of a rescued dog and a rescued fish swimming alongside each other.

Ripples encircled Sunny's body while she waded around the tall grass and lily pads. She looked so natural in the water and slightly like a seal, her coat slick and silvery. I called her name to get her to look at me for a picture with my phone, but then she came bolting out, shimmying her coat and sprinkling me with pond water.

She nestled into my lap and soaked my jean shorts. I scratched her under the chin and wanted to ask, *How did it feel, Sunny girl? The splash of your body barreling into the water? The sloshing of your tail back and forth? Did a fish brush against your leg? Had you ever swam before?*

Sunny looked at me for a moment as if trying to understand my thoughts. An orange butterfly flew above Sunny's head, lackadaisical in comparison to two hummingbirds buzzing about. I grazed my hand on Sunny's back, the bumpy edges of her spine that I used to count almost gone.

Except for the sound of water trickling from a nearby fountain, the place was silent. The blue sky held a beaming sun that made the pond reflective and the water sparkle. The beauty of the place deeply humbled me. *God, what I had hoped for was so much smaller than this.*

Dog bones were scattered in the yard and I handed one over to Sunny. She began to chew, her lips and paws doused in drool. I told her that I hated how she couldn't have bones at the shelter, but she couldn't have cared less now, with such a delicious rawhide between her paws. She gnawed on the bone as though using her whole body.

While she chomped away, I didn't have to be smart or wise. I didn't have to say and do the right things. I wasn't expected to be entertaining or amusing. I was perfectly myself and nothing was about to steal my life. Not my mind. Not my past. Not food.

Joy sat in my throat like an egg resting on a spoon, quiet and fragile, but real.

WHEN I LEFT that day, the terror and desperation that Sunny normally displayed at my leaving were gone. In fact, she barely noticed. Chip took a few pictures of us out back on the deck together, but the puppy in Sunny wanted to play. There were other dogs to play with, birds to chase, trees to sniff, bones to chew. While I pulled out of the driveway, she ran through the trees back to the house, clouds of red dirt rising up after her paws, her broken tail wagging in the wind.

Once down the mountain, I drove straight to the ocean. I felt the need to stop at the beach, to step outside and feel the Malibu breeze, to take a minute and thank the universe for its mercy and small surprises.

When I parked and tiptoed on the blazing hot sand toward the water, I thought of how life once was.

So many nights, I stared out at the inky black ocean, believing that if I could only learn how to eat again and keep my hands out of my throat, that would be enough. I prayed hard and desperately to God and the sun and the moon and the ocean and the universe and every shelter dog I'd ever met, as if they were all genies, that I wouldn't ask for anything more.

But perhaps God isn't a collection of genies, and perhaps it's okay to hope for more than relief. To hope big. To hope for Sunny's limitless capacity to love.

I stepped into the water and felt tiny shells and rocks tickle the bottoms of my feet. A fish or a piece of seaweed brushed up against me. Waves came rushing in and out, in and out. I took a few steps deeper, until the water was up to my thighs. The sun melted into shades of glistening purple. My toes clenched and unclenched in the sand, which was wet, like mud.

EPILOGUE

Two years later . . .

ON SUMMER SOLSTICE of 2014, Danny and I got married at his parents' vineyard and winery, Kohill, in the mountains of Ramona Valley, California. My father, who returned to drinking shortly after he was released from jail, wasn't there.

At the end of an aisle adorned with ivory flowers in glass wine bottles, I held my mother's hand. The country song "Bless the Broken Road" played from two tall black speakers, and Mom and I began walking toward the handsome man I was about to marry. Vast green mountains faded into a pale blue sky behind him.

Then a strong wind came. I'm not sure where the wind came from, or why it decided to swallow up my processional song, but the music stopped abruptly. Mom and I froze and she squeezed my hand. Almost two hundred guests looked awkwardly at us, and then as if someone told them to do it in unison, they stared blankly at the crackling speakers.

But I didn't worry. My own music played on repeat inside me, a song about how it could rain or I could cry or trip and fall on my face, and it would all be okay. A song of radical, untouchable joy.

Then the wind calmed and a bird flew over us and the wedding music came back on, though still ear-bending and scratchy. Mom smiled and looked into my watery eyes. I hooked my arm in hers, and we continued walking.

Grandma Elsie, dressed head to toe in sparkly purple, beamed in the front row. My sister stood a few feet in front of her in a long, cornflower-blue gown, where after Mom gently placed my hand in Danny's and kissed us both, Julie held my flowers.

Beneath an arch filled with poetry, vineyard greens, and peonies, I didn't marry Prince Charming.

I married a man who let me cry on his shoulder when I packed my bags for rehab seven years earlier.

And who once looked into my eyes and told me I was stronger than I knew, and turned out to be right.

And who adored four-legged creatures as much as I did, and who supported my dreams of becoming a writer, and who, every year for the past five years, sat in a circle among mostly women, applauding when I received another token for twelve months free from bulimia.

Prince Charming is boring and predictable and the last thing on earth I ever needed. What I needed was Danny. A man who infused my heart with laughter. A man who once gave me a copper lotus flower necklace.

A man who taught me that when life falls apart, love doesn't have to.

SPEAKING OF LOVE, it was about eight months after our wedding that Danny and I arrived at Project Unleashed for a reunion with Alicia, Chip, Sunny, and her family.

I stood at the bottom of a stone staircase near a collection of blue, mustard-yellow, and red birdhouses. The sugary white flower beds and lush trees all around me shined more than usual after the previous day's rain. Sunny, now renamed Sweet Pea, was playing with other rescued dogs in the yard at the top of the steps.

Danny wanted to capture our reunion on camera, so he went up the stairs in front of me. I heard him meet Sweet Pea's new family, who adopted her about a month after she arrived at Project Unleashed, and whom I'd met once before in Los Angeles.

Brandy, a stylish event planner, was giving Sweet Pea a healthy dose of Hollywood pampering and immeasurable love every day. Olive was a fifteen-year-old miniature greyhound who Sweet Pea treated like a long-lost sister from the very start. Brandy posted pictures on Instagram of the two of them cuddling in a plush bed, or sharing a seat in Brandy's open convertible, or gazing lovingly into each other's eyes while tucked under the same blanket. Despite their major age and size differences, the two were inseparable.

"Are you ready?" Danny shouted from the yard.

"Yes!" I shouted from the bottom of the stairs.

And at the sound of my voice, one word, Sweet Pea came barreling down the stairs, skipping one and sometimes two at a time, the wind blowing her floppy ears and her black lips back. I gasped at the sight of her and knelt down with open arms.

Within seconds she was at the bottom step. She jumped up on her hind legs and bear-hugged me, one front leg on each of my shoulders. Her tail, which looked much healthier, wagged behind her in ecstasy. My head leaned over her shoulder and I kissed the side of her neck. My hands stroked her flanks, her back, beneath her ears.

"How's my sweet girl?" I said.

She panted and looked right into my eyes. I had seen plenty of ridiculously happy and affectionate Sweet Pea pictures over the years, but still, I was unprepared for such an exuberant greeting. I'm not sure if a dog can glow in the way a person does after being kissed, but she seemed to be glowing like that. And I'm sure I was, too.

She came down on all fours and swirled around herself a few times, a doggy joy dance. Then she leaned into me with her flanks. Her brown eyes squinted in the sunlight, her pink tongue hung loosely out of her mouth. She moved her gaze to my right hand, where she licked every finger, and then my thumb again, just in case she hadn't given it adequate attention.

Sweet Pea was still a small dog for her breed—perhaps malnourishment impacted her growth, or perhaps she was always meant to be small. One thing was for sure: the size of her body reflected nothing about the enormity of her spirit.

Of course she wasn't concerned with how the moment was supposed to look, or freezing it in time with videos and photos. She was concerned with what mattered, the love she remembered. The voice she still, after all this time, knew well.

I thought about how I used to talk to her in that barren kennel, and then I remembered her weak body, her broken tail, her bloody head. I started to think about what a tragic loss it would have been for her to have not made it. But then Sweet Pea licked my neck. She swirled around herself again and began making her way up the steps, pausing to look back at me, as if to say, *Aren't you coming? This yard is really something to rave about!*

I glanced up the stairs and Danny shrugged and smiled. The

iPhone video he took is mostly of the ground, and in the background Danny says, "Ready? Oh, shit. Wait! Well, okay."

Danny has always arrived at that "Well, okay" place sooner
than me. Acceptance, I believe it is called—that song that
played inside me on my wedding day. But I'm learning to listen
for it better. I'm learning to embrace this beautiful, sometimes
incomprehensible world, and refrain from calling it good or
bad. To open my mind and immerse myself in the flow of
things, where mystery and irony and true wisdom live.

Because the truth is, while bulimia is a devastating illness I
would wish upon no one, it has taught me about the fragility
of life and the vital need for compassion. Today, I'm quick to
love and throw my arms around any girl who has ever stared at
a puddle of her own vomit and questioned the point of her life.
Or who has ever let a Photoshopped image on a glossy magazine preach to her about her own self-worth, her own beauty.
Or who has ever been afraid to face the pain and suffering,
within and outside of herself.

Today, I'm quick to love.

In fact, before this Project Unleashed reunion, I went over
to a stranger's house around midnight. My number was on
a hotline for people suffering from eating disorders, and this
woman called me after having puked a dozen times that day. In
her downtown apartment, she buried her head on my shoulder
and asked me why she couldn't stop. She asked me if her life
would always be this way. She was in her early twenties.

I told her what others once told me, which was that she was
not a bad person, but a sick person. I told her that healing from
an eating disorder is a personal journey—the medicine is whatever reminds you that you do in fact want to live, and that you
are worthy and capable of love.

I told her that shelter dogs were my medicine, and she needed to find hers. I said that I would do all I could to help her try to find it.

Because if I know anything at all, it's that giving saves lives. Especially the giver's.

AFTERWORD

A WORD ON PIT BULLS

NO DOGS ARE more persecuted or discriminated against than pit bulls, and no dogs have taught me more about resilience and forgiveness than they have. Pit bulls are my four-legged sanctuaries, my therapists, my healers, my beefy love-bugs, my comedians, my joy, and my motivation to keep fighting. I'm hopeful that after years of misperceptions and myths about the breed, we are coming closer to the day when breed discrimination is a thing of the past. Regardless of what we look like or where we come from, all of us deserve a fair shot at demonstrating the truth of who we are. Dogs are individuals and should be judged based on their individual behavior, not their breed.

Adopting an animal of any kind is a serious decision, and pit bulls are strong dogs who require owners committed to providing for their physical, mental, and emotional needs. But when a loving pit bull finds the right, loving home, families are often shocked by their devotion, resiliency, and affection. If not for the media bias that shifted public perception in the eighties (see next section), this wouldn't come as such a surprise. While it's true that some pit bull type dogs were originally bred to fight, centuries ago, it is also true that they have long been popular family dogs known to prefer the company of people to anything else. Today thousands of pit bulls across America are pet-assisted therapy dogs, search-and-rescue dogs, educators, athletes, and just all-around wiggly-butt cuddle machines.

If you take away anything from this book, please let it be this: don't pass by a pit bull at your local shelter because of their breed. You might just miss out on love and resilience beyond measure.

REFLECTIONS ON PIT BULLS, FROM BAD RAP ORGANIZATION

Please visit www.badrap.org for all things pit bulls, and to take a stand against breed discrimination!

A BRIEF HISTORY OF THE BREED

Created in the UK:

A dog (Olde English bulldog) that looked much like today's American bulldog was originally used in the 1800s in the British Isles to "bait" bulls. These matches were held for the entertainment of the struggling classes; a source of relief from the tedium of hardship. In 1835 bull baiting was deemed inhumane and became illegal, and dogfighting became a popular replacement. Soon a new bulldog was created by crossing the Olde English bulldog with terriers to create smaller, more agile dogs. The best fighters were celebrated and held up as heroes for their courage and fortitude during battle. At the same time, bite inhibition toward humans was encouraged through selective breeding, so gamblers could handle their dogs during staged fights. Partially because of these early breeding efforts, which frowned on "man biters," pit bulls gained a reputation for their trustworthy nature with humans.

History in America:

When immigrants came to America, their dogs came with them as a part of the family. In early America, pit bulls were not valued much for their fighting abilities. Instead, they were used to protect homes from predators and helped out on the farm. Children were entrusted in their care, and they quickly became a well-loved and important part of a developing nation.

As cities sprang up, pit bulls remained a prominent part of the American culture. Americans admired this breed for qualities that they likened to their own: friendly, brave, hard-working, worthy of respect. Pit bulls were thought of less as pit fighters and more as "regular dogs." They show up in hundreds of turn-of-the-century photos, flanked by loving family members. Early advertisements, posters, and magazines began to use the image of the all-American dog, including Buster Brown, whose companion was a pit bull.

Our first canine war hero, Sergeant Stubby, was a pit bull, a proud mascot of courage and loyalty in World War I. The pit bull was also a favorite dog among politicians, scholars, and celebrities. Helen Keller, Theodore Roosevelt, and *Our Gang's* Little Rascals all had pit bulls.

Pit bulls are beautiful in their variety, but their most appealing features are their inner qualities. Strength, confidence, a sense of humor, and a zest for life are all hallmarks of the breed. They also tend to be sensitive and get their feelings hurt easily. Properly socialized dogs are quite affectionate and friendly, even with strangers, and therefore do not make good guard dogs. They're intelligent and eager to please and tend to remain playful throughout their lives. While some can be low-key "couch potatoes," many others need a job to channel their enthusiasm and energy. Today many excel in dog sports, search-and-rescue work, drug and bomb detection, and as therapy dogs.

A LONELY TWIST IN THE ROAD

While large numbers of pit bull–type dogs in this country live out their lives as cherished family companions, many not so fortunate suffer from man-made shortcomings, including unspeakable cruelties, the socioeconomic pressures of underresourced owners, and the relentless biases and discrimination of an ill-informed public. Pit bulls began to be exploited through dogfighting in greater numbers in the 1980s and were soon associated with poverty, "urban thugs," and crime. The media capitalized on fears of a modern-day werewolf by promoting stereotypical images, and the reputation of the entire breed was dragged down with sensationalistic headlines and damaging myths and untruths.

Dogfighting is now a felony in all fifty states and arrests have increased, and many people now work to restore the dog's image to its rightful place as an American tradition. But even the most responsible owners still struggle to keep their dogs safe from discrimination and harm. The larger threats to the dogs are much more insidious and mainstream than even the threat of dogfighting, and result in an unforgivable prejudice that condemns countless pit bulls to homelessness and an early death.

STILL HEROES

Despite the societal pressures many of the dogs and their owners endure, one thing rings true: the pit bull that was once courageous enough to save human lives on a World War I battlefield now utilizes that same bravado to accomplish modern-day feats—including surviving conditions that would drive most humans to madness. There are no greater contemporary examples of this resiliency and ability to bounce back from darkness than the dogs rescued from Michael Vick's Bad Newz Kennels. Despite the unthinkable physical and emotional horrors these dogs endured, thirty-eight dogs and counting have found loving homes since the rescue. The media couldn't help but notice these remarkable stories of recovery, and the public happily embraced them. Twenty years after the breed took its first major PR hit in the media, *Sports Illustrated* returned to show us a different face of the dog, one that invokes sympathy and even surprise from a re-educated public. Breed enthusiasts celebrated the historic *Sports Illustrated* issue and hailed it as a sign of a welcome change in the landscape.

In loving and committed homes, pit bulls dazzle us with unmistakable charms. It's not hard to see that the original Hero Dog is still alive and well in the show ring, in the various dog sport competitions, in law enforcement work, in our homes, and even in the saddest of places in our urban shelters.

The rescued pit bulls at BAD RAP accurately reflect that same original spirit of tail wagging resiliency. To welcome a new member into your family, or to learn more about this beautiful breed, visit www.badrap.org.

ABOUT PROJECT UNLEASHED

"I relate to the powerless animal, I am a survivor of violence. But I've found my way, seeing through the eyes of my offender, I have felt true forgiveness and love, and that has been liberating and humbling."

—Project Unleashed founder Alicia Stevenson
www.projectunleashed.org

For many adolescents growing up on the streets of Los Angeles, the qualities of empathy and compassion are rarely celebrated. In fact, these values are synonymous with vulnerability and weakness, and are dispelled with as a matter of survival.

Project Unleashed is a program that recognizes the phenomenon of canine-human connection as a powerful means to quickly reintroduce empathy and compassion for those who have lost them.

The program pairs at-risk, incarcerated, or inner-city youth with rescued shelter dogs, and the pairs work together on a journey of collaboration and healing. The kids work with a dog trainer and a therapist as they learn how to train and care for animals who have been marginalized, neglected, and abused in ways that these kids can understand. Observers of the program, for instance case managers from our partner organizations, recognize the magic that lives in this connection, and its ability to transform an individual in a remarkably short amount of time. The participants gain a new understanding of themselves and the world around them.

Some of the program elements covered: Laws that protect animals against dogfighting and other animal cruelty. The importance of spay/neuter, which prevents animal overpopulation and overcrowding at city shelters, annually leading to the deaths of millions of healthy, lovable, adoptable animals. Participants learn brain science, the similarities and differences of human and animal behavior, pack mentality, and human group mentality. They learn daily needs for the type of animal in their care, and training of that animal, using positive reinforcement.

Ultimately, Project Unleashed's goal is to impart a greater sense of self, and from that comes empathy, and empathy can be a very powerful, practical thing.

ACKNOWLEDGMENTS

MY HEART IS full of gratitude for the many who helped bring this book to life. Thank you to my agent, Lisa Bankoff, and to my editor, May Chen, for believing in this book in its early stages and for all of your amazing support along the way. Thank you also to the team at HarperCollins for all of your dedication and hard work!

Mike Magnuson, you are the greatest teacher that's ever been. Thank you for pushing me so much further than I ever thought I could go. I agree with Rocks—you are truly amazing. This book wouldn't exist if not for your invaluable support and guidance.

Katie Martin, my brave and beautiful friend, thank you for being my other half on this journey. Jim Willwerth, words can't express how lucky I feel to have learned from you—thanks for your edits, your humor, your friendship. Camille Forbes, I love you as a sister. You are one of the most generous, bighearted, beautiful people I know.

I'm infinitely grateful for my friends and teachers at Pacific University, and especially Mike Magnuson, Katie Martin, Debra Gwartney, Pam Houston, Deb Becker, Amy Shannon, Carrie Targhetta, Charlotte O'Brien, Crystal Beavers, and

Tiffany Hauck. Carrie, thank you for your beautiful thoughts and for helping me to cross the finish line! Thanks also to Joyce Actor and the GLAWS memoir group in West Hollywood! Gerry Moylan, this book is all the better because of you—thank you.

There are too many special friends and family members who have supported me over the years to thank in these pages, but I believe you know who you are, and that your love has meant everything.

Thank you to Dr. Karla Materna, Rosewood Centers for Eating Disorders, BBA, and all those who have guided me on my journey toward healing. Thank you to Kerry and John at La Muse for providing a sacred space to write. Thank you to Mike, Aurora, and Kristi Kopp for encouraging my dreams and always being there for me.

Thank you to the San Diego Humane Society and SPCA for your ongoing support and all-around incredibleness on behalf of animals. Laura Coburn and Candice Eley, my dear friends and fellow animal lovers—you mattered more than you'll ever know. Laura Maloney, Michael Baehr, and Elkie Wills: thank you for being my inspiration.

Thank you to all those who helped to rescue Sweet Pea, especially Lisa Shapiro, Sherman Baylin, Alicia Stevenson, Chip Warren, Blaine Cline, and Brandy Greenleaf. Brandy, thanks for giving Sweet Pea the home of her dreams. Jen Bergren and Leslie Culver, thank you for going above and beyond to capture the moment!

Thank you to all those at BAD RAP, especially Tim Racer and Donna Reynolds, for your life-saving work in support of pit bull–type dogs everywhere.

From the bottom of my heart, thank you, Mom, for always supporting my dreams. You're my angel. Grandma Elsie, there isn't enough sugar in the world to show how much I love you. Dad, thank you for supporting this book—I love you and pray for your recovery.

Julie, I carry your heart always.

Danny, your love is the greatest gift I've ever known. I'm the luckiest girl in the world to call you mine. Thank you for your relentless support of this book, and for being my rock. I love you.

Thank you, God, for Your Love and Light.

Thank you to Sweet Pea, Bella, Sugar, and the many shelter dogs who have loved me back to life.